Praise for *Veracity & Verse*

"James A. Forbes Jr. is an Isaiah of our time with a gifted ear to hear the voice of the Spirit, a golden tongue to proclaim the good news, an anointed pen to write the vision and make it plain. The Lord has given my mentor and friend, Dr. James A. Forbes Jr., a gifted ear to hear the voice of the Spirit, a golden tongue to proclaim the good news, and an anointed pen to write the vision and make it plain. These poems capture the energy and essence of his prophetic articulation across a lifetime of ministry. What a gift to have them gathered here in one place."
—Reverend Dr. William J. Barber II

"These spiritual reflections center and anchor us in times of change and upheaval. Flowing out of his ninety years of life, Jim provides spiritual reflections that center and anchor in times of change and upheaval. He leads us to the ground of hope, providing us with strength, courage, and a renewed commitment to believe and achieve the world that God intends."
—Reverend Dr. Yvonne Delk

"Dr. Forbes is a rare person, congruent through all aspects of his being."
—Nicki McClusky

"James A. Forbes Jr. is a spiritual genius, an intellectual giant, and a poetic titan! Like his legendary sermons over the past sixty-five years, these poems speak to our hearts, minds, and souls! He also has been a divine gift in my life!"

—Dr. Cornel West

"As a renowned preacher, Dr. Forbes's professional life has been well spent in offering others comfort, in times of despair; direction, in times of confusion; and hope for liberation, in times of social chastisement. He has done the same here, in written form, with this divinely inspired collection of poems. Dr. Forbes creatively addresses social issues like poverty and race in America, while humbly showing faithfulness to God, his creator, and fidelity to his precious family, God's gift to him. He shows gratefulness for God's providence and power, as well as pride in what others might deem social pejoratives. He is who he is, because God made him that way! My mentor, brother, and friend has brought together both rural North Carolina charm and Big Apple flare in a collection of poems that will be cherished for generations to come."

—Dr. Jonathan C. Augustine

"I am proud to endorse the rich collection of Dr. Forbes's inspiring poetry. Many of these poems he read to me over the phone when they were first written. I enthusiastically urge you to immerse yourself in his writing and be edified and transformed."

—Johnnetta B. Cole, PhD

"I have always thought of Dr. Forbes as a poet. His sermons and ministry offered us a way of seeing the world, ourselves, and our relationship to God in more expansive terms. That's what poets do. Now we have his poems. Art, wisdom, spiritual meditation between the pages of a book—a glimpse into the heart and spirit of this extraordinary man of God."

—Eddie S. Glaude Jr.

"Dr. James A. Forbes Jr. presents a work masterfully conceived in deep reflection. It is impossible not to take a mental flight into the depths of spirituality that Dr. Forbes's ministry and these poems represent in the annals of Christian theology. These poems and lamentations offer but a small insight into the depths of a towering figure of spirituality."

—Former Congressman Jesse Jackson Jr.

"A pastor to pastors, one of the fine theologians of our age, Reverend James A. Forbes Jr.'s captivating book of lyrical poems is not only a balm to the heart of the cries of the American nation, it is a stunning tribute to the principles of truth, faith, gratitude, justice, and love through which he has lived his extraordinary life. It is a gift for us all."

—Sarah Lewis, PhD

"Dr. Forbes's near century of service has so much to teach us. This collection of poetry is spiritually nourishing and inspiring."

—Heather C. McGhee

"Legendary preaching poet Dr. James A. Forbes Jr. unveils his heart in poetic form to instigate a spiritual EKG of our own heart. He engages a wide range of human topics with the vulnerability, tenderness, and truth of divine love. His writing is a revelation of faith, hope, and love in words—faith in God, hope for the future, and love for others. Readers who digest this book will be fed with more than rhythmic words but holy bread from heaven."

—Reverend Dr. Luke A. Powery

"I am a man who believes that there is never too much room to call for freedom or let it call to us with its tremendous and tender sound. In this collection by Dr. Forbes, freedom is much more than the Ole English word that means the 'power of self-determination.' It walks, it sings, it groans, it bends itself toward justice, and bends its heart toward honesty; it burrows its way into every nook and cranny of our soul until we are one. For such a glorious elder as himself, to still be dreaming of freedom is more than just some parting note. It is the very oxygen that keeps our hearts going when our hearts weaken. This voice is wisdom walking forward. It's a gift."

—Danté Stewart

"Dr. Forbes has been my mentor and friend for many years. He has constantly sought to promote the gospel of peace, justice, and equality. America has never done well when she has ceased to seek to do the will of God. Dr. Forbes does that now. His work has been a steady infusion of energy in our work for justice and equality."

—Reverend Ambassador Andrew Young

VERACITY AND VERSE

Also by Rev. Dr. James A. Forbes Jr.

Whose Gospel? A Concise Guide to Progressive Protestantism

VERACITY & VERSE

Rev. Dr. James Alexander Forbes Jr.

A PREACHER'S
REFLECTIONS
& POEMS
ON FAITH
& TRUTH

Broadleaf Books
Minneapolis

VERACITY AND VERSE
A Preacher's Reflections and Poems on Faith and Truth

Copyright © 2025 James A. Forbes Jr. Published by Broadleaf Books. All rights reserved. Except for brief quotations in critical articles or reviews, no part of this book may be reproduced in any manner without prior written permission from the publisher. Email copyright@broadleafbooks.com or write to Permissions, Broadleaf Books, PO Box 1209, Minneapolis, MN 55440-1209.

29 28 27 26 25 24   1 2 3 4 5 6 7 8 9

Scripture quotations marked (KJV) are taken from the King James Version.

Library of Congress Cataloging-in-Publication Data

Names: Forbes, James A., Jr., author.
Title: Veracity & verse : a preacher's reflections and poems on faith and truth / the Rev. Dr. James A. Forbes, Jr.
Other titles: Veracity and verse
Description: Minneapolis, MN : Broadleaf Books, [2025] | Includes index.
Identifiers: LCCN 2024036267 | ISBN 9798889832416 (hardcover) | ISBN 9798889832799 (ebook)
Subjects: LCSH: Forbes, James A., Jr., | African American clergy--Biography. | Christian poetry, American. | American poetry--African American authors. | Christian life.
Classification: LCC BX6455.F67 V47 2025 | DDC 280/.4092 [B]--dc23/eng/20241122
LC record available at https://lccn.loc.gov/2024036267

Cover design by Broadleaf Books

Print ISBN: 979-8-8898-3241-6
eBook ISBN: 979-8-8898-3279-9

Printed in China.

LIST OF POEMS

My Family, Your Family	1
"Are All the Children In" Table Grace	14
The Spirit Is the Key to Community	16
Thank You, Thank You, Thank You	17
Ever Lasting Loving Kindness	18
Sharing Makes Us Happy	20
Freedom, Sweet Freedom	27
For Children Safe and Strong	28
We Have Come This Far by the Power of Prayer	29
If You Believe My Word	31
Imagine a World	35

A Hint of Freedom	40
You've Got to Stop Running	42
Determined to Be Good Soil	45
I'll Do Whatever You Want Me to Do	47
Thank You for My D-N-A	51
Drop the Thought of Dropping Out	53
A Way Was Made	54
We Are One in Your Spirit	59
On the Way to Freedom	60
Spirituality	64
Holy Spirit, Lead Me, Guide Me	65
The Fruit of the Spirit Is	65
A Message of Quantum Love from God	67
The Courage to Be Who We Are	70
How Can You?	72
The Divine Reprimand	74
Thoughts at a Desegregated Lunch Counter	83
We Shall Overcome, for Sure	88
Seeing Myself Through the Eyes of God	94
God's Dream of the World	97
Sweet Communion	99

Beautiful Nappy Hair — The Miracle in the Black Hair Salon	103
What Kind of Love Are You Dreaming Of?	107
The Beautiful Truth About Naomi and Ruth	109
Thus, Saith the Lord	120
We All Can Be Philanthropists	121
Excellence! Excellence! Excellence!	132
Doctor, Tell Me Why?	137
I'm Living in Hope	138
Golden Moments of Kindness	140
In This Special Holy Place	141
An Ode to Me, We, and Thee	142
Everybody Let's Get Ready	143
Thank You Jesus for Being There for Me	145
Never Give Up on You	146
LOVE MY CHILDREN	148
Thank You for Making and Mending Me for Love — a Prayer	149
Whether or Not	155
Zion, Beautiful Zion	156

A Melody of Praise	157
A Conversation with Our Nation About Race	163
Who Do We Think We Are?	165
Rap Response	166
No Time for Foolishness	166
When True Healing Has Begun	168
Love's Response to the Crisis of the Nation	170
When God is Acknowledged as God Again	172
God's Dream of the World	173
A Sighting of the Hand of God	174
I'll Be with You 'til the End of Time	176
The More Perfect Voter	179
Vote NO! to Hate	181
Voter Suppression: A Punishable Offense	181
Will the Supreme Court Honor Our Constitution?	182
Census Sensibility	183
The Winning Vote	183
Get on the Path	184

All Americans Together	188
Koolibah, Koolibah	190
Community—Humanity at Its Best	191
Song of the Heavens	193
Woe unto Those Who Desecrate the Earth	195
Other Wonders of the World	195
A Little Bit of Heaven	201
Go Forth	207

FOREWORD

Poetry is when emotion has found its thought, and the thought has found its words.

—Robert Frost

THE POET IS unique among the artists. They use human language to paint emotion and images around the yearnings and urges of the human heart and soul. Language is limited and the poet, with this knowledge, attempts to find unconventional ways to capture the uncapturable.

Robert Frost conveys this yearning when he states, "A poem begins as a lump in the throat, a sense of wrong, a homesickness, a love sickness."[1] Poetry attempts to communicate what cannot fully be communicated, such as the ever-expansive ideas of love, grace, and mercy. We have definitions of these words, but it takes a poet to convey the depth of meaning. This is why the Old Testament prophets were viewed as poets, stewards of sacred mysteries, called to paint with sonic and oral brushes upon the canvas of the human heart. The prophet and poet seeks to illuminate the sacred nature of life and light a path for a better future.

Dr. James A. Forbes Jr. has been, throughout his ministry, the preeminent Pentecostal prophetic poet of our age. He combines the urgency of Amos and Jeremiah with the Blues sensibility of Langston Hughes and August Wilson. Every time he paints poetic imagery on the canvas of our imagination, his distinctive voice calls us to account, yet offers a loving hope of what can be if we dare to return to our spiritual roots.

Our nation deeply needs prophetic poets who offer a vision of a nation that is yet to be. What makes Dr. Forbes's poetry potent is his unflinching analysis of history, devoid of any romanticism or nostalgia. We see the fullness of America with her aspirations, bruises, beauty, horror, and hopes.

---

[1] "Robert Frost." Poetry Foundation, Poetry Foundation, www.poetryfoundation.org/poets/robert-frost, Accessed 5 October 2024.

In this moment of history, we have propaganda masquerading as "truth telling," a refusal to examine any of the tragic moments of our history while simultaneously holding an image of a nation that never existed.

Dr. Forbes is our poet and prophet, and the words he offers in this collection shall challenge, comfort, afflict, soothe, and call all who read to account. Not unlike his spiritual ancestor, Jeremiah, this man has a fire shut up in his bones. Let this poet speak and set us free!

—Rev. Dr. Otis Moss III

PREFACE

I AM SO comfortable as a preacher and I write sermons all the time, but I tend to be visited in my quiet time, and sometimes even in the night. It is during the quiet time and in the night that these valuable fragments awaken me through poetry. It is not so much that I am a poet, but at times the fragmentary ideas find rhythm, and this rhythm is what I put together to share with you in this book, along with reflections as I look over my life.

I have included thoughts that have marinated through the day, that seek some kind of expression but lack a more permanent reservoir for meaning. After reflection, I recognize these poems can attest to what I hear and see, along with the struggles, joys, and imponderables that I confront occasionally and have determined something needs to be said. I have attempted to capture some of those thoughts, and I believe they come from a place that deserves serious reflection, as they are the bearers of insight that have life transforming or life enriching capacities.

Many of my poems were created in memory of the dedication my parents and church community had for moving forward and staying connected by the faith, hope, and love of God. The segregated South was the backdrop of our living; however, the love of God sustained us.

My sense is that these poems might pick up someone's spirit, they might deposit a resolution regarding some values, they might quicken someone to changes that they want to make, and they might nudge people toward a greater faithfulness to their own sense of integrity.

May these words from my heart and reflections on my life bless you on your journey.

My Family, Your Family

When the world was young, and the time
    had come
For children to laugh and play,
A plan was made to welcome them
And to guide them day by day.
Each child will have a family
For safe and tender care.
The family will be a place
Where children learn to share.

My family, your family with lots of love
    to spare
Will make this world a happy place for
    children everywhere.

All our dear kinfolk and our closest friends
Are part of our family.

We know each other's special names
And what fills our hearts with glee.
Some relatives share one big house,
And some live miles away.
But they still try to stay in touch
Through loving thoughts each day.

My family, your family with lots of love
    to spare
Will make this world a happy place for
    children everywhere.

When we all join hands in a family,
A beautiful strength is there
To build a home where everyone
Is thoughtful, kind, and fair.
In all the world, there is no place
More comforting than this,
A family where each child finds
A smile, a hug, a kiss.

My family, your family with lots of love
    to spare—
Will make this world a happy place for
    children everywhere.

The second of eight children and the eldest boy, I was born on September 6, 1935, in Burgaw, North Carolina. That's in Pender County, about twenty-five miles from Wilmington. My parents, James A. Forbes and Mabel Clemons Forbes, were dedicated to our family. We lived in a three-bedroom house on Bloodworth Street. I was a preacher's kid. I went to Sunday school. I sang in the choir of my father's church.

My daddy is James Alexander Forbes, and, of course, as we kids were born, he became Senior. He was born in Greenville, North Carolina, on March 19th, 1914, to Anna Little Forbes and Charlie Forbes. Anna Forbes is the only paternal grandparent we know because Charlie Forbes, who had raised five or six kids, had just disappeared, just walked away and left the family. We were told efforts were made to find him, and maybe somebody who reads this story will say, "We know where Charlie Forbes went," but our family traced him as best we could, and we do not know. My father was the second eldest and had to drop out of school to help take care of the family. He was in the sixth grade. He developed a sense of fatherly responsibility by helping his mother take care of the rest of the family. He was quite a young man when he took on this extra duty.

At a certain age, about seventeen years old, I think, he decided he was going to be a preacher. He accepted the call to ministry and became quite a popular preacher in North Carolina. The big problem was that he was what used to be termed a "bootleg" or "jackleg" preacher, meaning he didn't have any education and had not been thoroughly trained for the vocation. One of the churches Daddy served said, "We really like your preaching, but if you're gonna be our preacher, you're gonna have to get some education." So, having dropped out of school in the sixth grade, he enrolled in a high school correspondence course called the American School of Correspondence in Lansing, Illinois.

I remember, as a little boy, taking Daddy's lessons that he prepared at the dining room table and posting them in the mailbox, then picking up the letters from the mailbox when he got his grades back. He completed high school through correspondence having only gone to sixth grade. But he was sufficiently bright that after finishing high school by correspondence, he enrolled in college at Shaw University near where we lived in Raleigh, North Carolina. He graduated from Shaw around 1949, the head of his class, and decided to go further to get— what they called then—his "BD" or Bachelor of Divinity, which is now called MDiv, Master of Divinity. And if you can believe it, this man—my father—graduated from college about the same time as my other sisters and brothers because he had gone back to school as they were growing up.

In my family, the importance of earning an education was very clear. Just as morning is the first part of the day, the day isn't complete until you come to night. You *go* to school. College is as natural as morning is to night. In our family everybody managed to get beyond college. Most of us earned advanced degrees because education was one of the ways we honored our father. If you've got a daddy who, with eight kids, goes back to college, what excuse do you have not to find a way to complete your education?

As he pastored Providence United Holy Church in Raleigh, went to school preparing for his ministry degree, and raised eight children, he held a job working at the W. T. Grant department store. He was a porter and a candy salesman. This is very important: my father always viewed himself as not just working for somebody. Although he was a porter and a candy salesman, when the head of the store, Mr. Parsons, announced to the staff that he had just had a little baby girl, my father made a table with four chairs as a gift for the baby. Now, how do I know this? Because decades later, I preached at Memorial Drive Presbyterian Church in Houston, Texas. My name was on the street sign in front of the church. The sign built me up, announcing my sermon as a big occasion. A person named Mrs. Parsons came with her children and said, "I heard James Forbes was preaching. I am the daughter for whom a table and chairs were made by a James Forbes." Wherever her family moved, they could leave anything behind, she said, but they could never leave behind the table that someone she only knew by the name—James Forbes—had made for her. It was fascinating to live long enough to have that circle completed. My father was a Black man who showed his care for his employer, a white man. He was not a worker; he was a servant of God who showed love to whomever he could.

Eventually he became Bishop James A. Forbes Sr. of the United Holy Church of America. He was among the previous generation of Pentecostal preachers. He headed what they called the BTI, Bible Training Institute, then renamed the United Christian College in Goldsboro, North Carolina. There was a periodical for the denomination called *The Holiness Union* and my father was the head of that. He was an educator and great preacher who exemplified lifelong learning. He believed that if you give the Lord your whole self, you don't leave your head out. You say, "Lord, take my all." What about your brain? What about your mind? He was quite a visionary.

I don't know how my parents met. I would assume that it had to do with church, because like my father, O. C. Clemons, my mother's father, was a minister. He was a well-off Black tobacco farmer, and he gave money to build the Black school in town and led Clemons Grove

Pentecostal Church in Stokes, North Carolina. They used to call him Mr. Big Orange because he was a big man, the kind of guy who drove Buicks. Every year they'd come from the car dealer and get my grandfather's old Buick or Cadillac and bring him a new car because he had to have the latest. Rosa Clemons was his wife, my mother's mother, from what we know from the family cemetery across from Clemons Grove. I never knew her.

O. C. Clemons had a wonderful house that was like a mansion sitting in the middle of a field. It had gables. It had two outhouses that had some style about them. Isn't that something? An outhouse with style? The house had a large eating space, a living room that had glass doors and was used only for very, very, very special occasions. It was called the "dormy room." I don't know why he called it that. What dormy meant, I don't know. There were upstairs bedrooms for each member of the family and a wonderful kitchen. We all enjoyed coming home from the fields to see what Mama Ada—later on, his second wife, Ada Clemons—had prepared for us. It was a special place, a little bit of heaven down on earth, Grandpa's big house.

We all knew that we were once slaves. My name is Forbes, F-O-R-B-E-S. I was receiving an honorary doctorate at Fairleigh Dickinson University in Teaneck, New Jersey, and another person who was receiving an honorary degree was Malcolm Forbes. His was posthumous, so Robert Forbes was there to receive it. I teased him, asking, "Where are you from?"

"Pitt County [North Carolina]," he answered.

"Pitt County. The Forbeses were big plantation owners, I suspect. I think the way the name of the plantation was spelled at first was F-O-R-B-apostrophe-S, the Forb's, or F-O-R-B-E-S with an apostrophe at the end: the Forbes'. You can check it out. When emancipation came, you all removed the apostrophe, but we, we know that we were the Forbes."

He wiped the sweat from his brow.

"That's okay," I consoled him, and then said, "one of these days I'm going to develop the other Forbes Foundation. We had spiritual and moral capital that has made a contribution to the world as well. You'd be proud of the offspring of your foreparents' laborers."

Even though my mother's father was a big tobacco farmer, every one of us worked hanging and drying the leaves. Every summer when we were out of school in Raleigh, we'd pack up and go down to Stokes, to Grandpa's farm to help put in tobacco. Putting in tobacco means you get there in time to help the tobacco grow. As tobacco plants grow, in the middle edges between the leaves are extraneous growths. We called those suckles. Part of helping tobacco grow is to get there in time to "suckle tobacco." First, you walk through the tobacco field removing the extraneous growth, the little leaves that would sap the energy from the full tobacco leaf.

Second, you worm the tobacco. Tobacco worms look like caterpillars with a horn. Your job is to go through the field and take the worms off because they will eat up the leaves. We were human pesticides as we took the worms and put them in a cup or can.

When the tobacco was up, fully grown and ripe, we started the process of actually harvesting the tobacco. My grandfather, the farmer, knew when it was time. Everybody had a job. Our job was to "crap tobacco." That means we would start on the fields and take the first two or three leaves that were ripened. That first week, you take two or three leaves, large, green but beginning to yellow, and put them in a mule truck. A mule would be dragging the truck as you scurried to put the tobacco in, and then it dragged the truck to the shed or barn. In the tobacco barn, loopers would string the tobacco. They had a fancy way about it. They would string the tobacco so that the leaves would hang in the tobacco barn to be cured before they were ready to be taken to the warehouse and auctioned off at the best possible price.

Your job in this process depended upon how old you were. At first, you simply handed the tobacco leaves off the truck when it came in the barn to the ladies who were doing the looping. They'd take it from your small hands, with a gesture particular to tobacco loopers. When you got older, you got the chance to drive the mule truck. When you got a little older, you got to crap tobacco. Eventually you had a chance to hang the tobacco in the barns. You used what we called tier poles. The big job was having the opportunity to put the fire in. This was flue-cured tobacco. You put a fire in the barn to raise the temperature so that a progressive increase of the temperature would appropriately cure the tobacco. It needed to be just right. The more golden it is, the better price it brings at the market.

Tobacco barn was a fun time. It was relaxation at the end of the day, at the end of autumn. There was no market in town, not in Stokes. The cured tobacco would be taken to a larger town, to Greenville or to Rocky Mount.

A fascinating thing in my memory is something I experienced one night during tobacco harvesting season when I was eight or nine years old. You would stay awake because you had to watch the thermometer all night long to make sure the wood—this is before oil-cured furnaces were used—inside the barn stayed at the right temperature. One night I was sitting there, and as I watched the thermometer, I saw a cricket hopping, and hopping fast. A frog was after the cricket. The frog flicked out his tongue to catch the cricket. A Parmalee snake, at the very moment the frog flicks out his tongue to catch the cricket, swallows the frog whole. That said something to me about life.

O. C. Clemons's daughter, Mabel Clemons, was my mother. Preachers had the opportunity to meet the young ladies of churches where they preached after service. At one or the other's preaching campaigns for O. C. Clemmons–my father met my mother. They married at Holy Trinity United Holy Church in Greenville, North Carolina, and stayed in that general area. They became the proud parents of eight children: five daughters and three sons.

Mabel Clemons Forbes, in my earliest memory of my mother, is holding one of my younger siblings as the firemen are coming through our living room to go to the bathroom to put out a fire. I loved to see the sparkle at the end of the umbrella when you struck it against the pot belly stove. It gave off beautiful sparks and made a sound. This time the spark became a fire. I figured the best thing to do was to get this fire out of the house, so I took the lit umbrella to the bathroom, which had a curtain over the window. As I was pushing the fire out the window, the curtain caught on fire. Now the house was on fire. My mother was standing at the door. I must have been about four years old. It was a traumatic moment.

My mother was the manager of the household and specialized in raising us children and supporting the ministry of her husband. My mother also worked as a domestic for a white family on the other side of town. In addition to these duties, she served as the president of the PTA at the Crosby-Garfield Elementary School in Raleigh, North Carolina. She was honored to serve as the president of the Minister's Wives Alliance of Raleigh.

One evening the alliance was meeting at our home. My mother had prepared some Jell-O as part of the refreshments for the meeting. She diced sweet apples and sprinkled them in the Jell-O before placing it in the refrigerator to congeal.

At the end of the meeting, Mama came to the kitchen to get the Jell-O to serve to the ladies. When she pulled out the Jell-O, she discovered that someone had extracted most of the apples. I only intended to take a cube—or maybe two—but they were so delicious, I could not withstand the temptation. There was scarcely a cube left.

My mother was both embarrassed and heartbroken. I will never forget the look of hurt on her face. She had to scramble to find alternative refreshments for the waiting alliance women.

That night, I went to bed before my mother had a chance to confront me. I knew she knew I was the thief. The next morning, with haste—because I didn't know what she was going to do to me—I got ready for school, had some cereal for breakfast, picked up my book bag, and headed for the door.

My mother, with a look of forgiving grace, gave me my lunch bag, kissed me on my forehead, and said, "Have a nice day." I will never forget that look of forgiving grace on my mother's face.

My childhood home had three bedrooms and many beds, but we had only one dining room table. We used every leaf in the table to seat us all. At dinner, Mama often began with a little ritual. When we were finally ready to say grace, she would ask, "Are all the children in?" We had to look around because with a family of our size, plus the guests that often joined us, we might not notice if somebody was missing. If we observed that somebody was missing, we were to speak up: "Fix a plate for _____." Then, we were permitted to say grace, but we could not fill our plates with food until we first prepared a plate for the missing member. That extra plate of food went into the oven of the old woodburning stove to keep it warm until the missing person arrived.

My mother raised us to know that the first act after grace, the first thing we must do as our expression of gratitude for the blessing of God, was to prepare a plate for those not yet at the table. Her ethic of love, of preparing a portion of the feast for others before we could enjoy it ourselves, became a part of my consciousness before I even thought about it, before I went to seminary, and before I was a minister.

In my 915 South Bloodworth Street home, I learned the values and rituals of gratitude and generosity that lie at the core of my understanding of the Christian gospel.

God's good news is that the one dining room table is big enough for every human being because Jesus Christ is the host of the table. He makes sure everyone is included; he turns no one away from the feast.

The feast is, of course, far more than one good meal a day, though there are far too many in the world who do not get even one good meal a week. The feast is abundant life, promised by Jesus Christ and delivered through the Holy Spirit. That Spirit must inspire Christians to assure everyone that they are invited to God's table. We must ask the critical question: "Are all the children in?" Let us commit to making sure all are at the table.

"Are All the Children In" Table Grace

Kind and loving Parent of all humankind,
We thank You that even before You
    created us,

You made food enough to spare
For our nourishment and care.

May we remain ever grateful
For all You have provided for us.
And forever mindful and responsive
To the needs of others.

Bless the food and fellowship we share
and Your children everywhere.
In the spirit of Your love, we pray.

Amen.

Also, while we were at the table, there was another ritual in our family. When something significant had happened for any one of us—whether Mom had just been elected as the president of the PTA, or whether Dad had gotten an assignment at the college of our denomination, or whether someone had won the jabberwocky contest for talent—the family ritual was to take five to ten minutes to do what we called "make over" that person. Once the announcement was made of the significant accolade, we made a fuss over the one who had been honored, for when one is honored, all are honored.

Also, at the dinner table, we had to make a report on our extended "visited" members, those in our extended family—the sick, elderly, shut in.

My task was, at least once a week, to visit Mother Williamson who lived on Bledsoe Avenue, and Mother Lassiter who lived on Oberlin Road. They were old and infirmed, and my responsibility was to go by to see if they needed anything. Mom said, "To be family, is to care and share and to look out for one another. They are our family."

Of course, sometimes there was a bonus for going to visit our "extended family" members. The elderly would offer me sweets or money. Mom said, "If they ask you what it costs to go shopping for them or to bring what they needed, you must always say, 'Nothing.' And if they insist, say, 'Whatever you mind to give me.'"

This was the nature of being at Mama's dinner table. In fact, she indicated that if we would do what she taught us, not only would we have the joy of receiving gratitude from members of the extended family, but, "Even God will smile," she said, "and when God smiles, there is peace and justice and joy."

The Spirit Is the Key to Community

The Spirit is the key to community
Where love and justice flow like streams
Where the people work together for the common good
To make our cities safe for dreams.

The Spirit sets us free from anxiety
About our neighbors far and near.
When we learn to welcome strangers, greeting them as friends
No longer are we bound by fear.

The Spirit sees the world as a
> neighborhood.
The Spirit yearns for wars to cease
So, the Spirit forms a circle of freedom-
> loving friends

To claim the world for hope and peace.
Spirit of community draws us close to Thee,
Helps us to see the beauty within diversity.
Begins with me, my friends, each neighborhood and nation,
Fulfills the dream you had in mind the first day of Creation.
We are building for the future, may the Spirit fill each heart
Then we will not let our differences tear our souls apart.
For we know that we are family, all God's children great and small.
Let's become that new community we have heard the Spirit call.

Thank You, Thank You, Thank You

Jesus sat by the well that hot and humid day.

The journey had been long, he had to pass that way.
Along came a woman bearing a water pot.
Would Jesus befriend her? Custom says, "Cert'nly not!"

Jews and Samaritans were divided by race.
What mattered most to him was her desperate case.
Forgiving all her sins, Jesus did not condemn.
Grace set her fully free as God's love flowed through Him.

Chorus
Unconditional love is the heart of the Gospel.
    It was in the beginning, will be so in the end.
God's love fills my heart with the spirit of praise.
Thank You, Thank You, Thank You—for the rest of my days.

Ever Lasting Loving Kindness

With everlasting loving kindness
I will always stand by you,

Giving you favor in barren seasons
Even when faithful friends are few.

You may, at times, have felt my anger
Humiliated by my wrath.
That was then, but this is now
Begin to walk the golden path.

Rejoice like mothers at the birthing
Of precious bundles of bright sunshine
Accept the pain as God sent angels
Announcing the gift of love divine.

Enlarge your tent, hang new curtains
Lengthen your chords, strengthen your stakes
Set your eyes toward my holy mountain
Walk right through the pearly gates.

Take possession of your blessings
Sapphires, rubies, and crystals too
There's no weapon that can harm you
I'll be there to see you through.

Chorus
Everlasting loving kindness, Everlasting loving kindness

Everlasting loving kindness, I will always stand by you.

Everlasting loving kindness, Everlasting loving kindness

Everlasting loving kindness, I will see you through.

Sharing Makes Us Happy

I made Heaven so happy today,
Receiving God's love and giving
it away.
When I looked up, Heaven smiled
at me.
Now I'm so happy, can't you see?

Sharing makes me happy, makes Heaven happy too.
Sharing lifts your spirit and brings the best from you.
Sharing sends a ray of hope to places needing care.
Sharing makes us neighbors—God's children everywhere.
I'm happy, look at me.
I'm happy, can't you see?

Sharing makes me happy,
Makes Heaven happy too.

I'm happy, look at me.
I'm happy, can't you see?
Let me share my happy, loving smile
with you.

MY MOTHER MANAGED to go to the ninth grade and was a wonderful leader in our community; she was a domestic. Dad was a full-time pastor by the time he reached Raleigh and was no longer working at W. T. Grant. My mother, with seven kids, and finally eight, would get up, get us ready to go to school, then—after getting us off to school—would take a back seat on the bus and go across town to work for a white family as a domestic. She had to take care of the family she worked for because the mother of *that* family was a working mother. She worked at Sears, Roebuck and Co. as a receptionist. My mother made thirty-five dollars a week: five days a week, seven dollars a day. Somewhere we learned that that other working mother whose house and family Mama was taking care of, was making over a hundred dollars a week. One working mother was paid a hundred dollars a week and another one thirty-five. I knew something must be wrong with the system. My mother was a queen. She was so magisterial and so caring, so blessed of God, so used by God, I was perplexed. Something was wrong, I thought.

Do you remember when you first became aware of race? My parents did so much to protect us from the jagged edges of segregated society that we learned to live with on our side of town. We were aware that things were different. The most serious manifestation of that difference was in school. For example, when you went to school, you went to the book room to pick up books at a particular time. We'd see that all the books had first been used by people across town at the white school. We didn't see any new books. All the books were already used by the white kids across town. We were aware of that.

I was a young adult when Central High was desegregated. The confrontation at the doors of Central High was disturbing, but it was not surprising to me. Racial conflict has been a fact of life for as long as I can remember. I have tried to recall the moment I discovered that some of us were Black and others were white. I had no such initial moment. Just as fish are already in the water and are unable to take notice of their habitat, race was the context in which I was born and raised, and segregation was the way things were. Life came in two basic varieties in my hometown—Black and white. It seemed to be the nature of things that these two groups lived in separate parts of town, went to separate schools and churches, had a different network of social contacts, and enjoyed well-defined boundaries of racial distancing. The main distinction marking their difference was that whites were assumed to be superior and that Blacks were a lesser breed of humanity. The pattern was so clearly established that we hardly noticed unless the protocols were violated and the boundaries were breached.

If Black toddlers wandered over to white water fountains or a Black child rushed toward the white restroom or a Black teenager sat at a lunch counter expecting to be served, their parents would quickly explain to them that Blacks and whites did not use the same facilities. Black kids who sat down at the front of the bus had to be instructed about the seating arrangements, and if the weather was cold, they could take comfort from the fact that they were closer to the warmth of the motor in the back of the bus.

Sooner or later the inevitable questions were asked, I suspect, on both sides of town. Why? Why can't we play together? Why can't we go to the same schools? On the Black side of town, kids asked, "Why do we have to sit in the balcony at the movie theater?" I wonder if the white kids asked their parents, "Why do they have to sit up there and we sit down here?" I am not sure what they were teaching in the white section of town, but the answers in my community were not satisfying. Instead, they were rather stoic resignations to the way things were, and our parents probably urged compliance for the sake of safety and survival. Sometimes there were muted protests: "They think they are better than we are." And other times resentment boiled over into acts of violence against the oppressive "etiquette" of race relations. Generally speaking, my community devised strategies for both endurance and for sustaining the dream that one day justice would prevail and the equal worth of all citizens would be affirmed.

By the time I reached adolescence I was highly sensitive to racist behavior and thinking. For example, our local radio station carried an editorial every morning. The commentator was Jesse Helms, who later became a senator from North Carolina. I remember distinctly that there were never any comments that affirmed my family, my church, or me. Always he seemed to speak against my people, against poor Negroes, against the oppressed. "My God!" I asked, "What is it with people who use their race as a dividing wall or a security blanket?" What is it that makes them so insecure that they cannot even trust God, whom they claim to worship? Pray for them, Jesus says.

All these years later, I still pray for those who think security comes from their own race, their lifestyle, their political party, their sexual orientation, their wealth, their theology, or their nation. I pray for those who wrap themselves in a blanket of their own particular identities and block out the warmth and light of God's grace. In them, the Spirit dies, the soul is impoverished, and love is increasingly confined and smothered in a blanket of fear.

Freedom, Sweet Freedom

Freedom, sweet freedom, the love of my life
Releasing my soul from hatred and strife.
Being free is a beautiful, world class fashion
Promoting justice, peace, and compassion.

Freedom restores our true humanity.
Fortifies our hearts with integrity.
Freedom helps us see our sisters and brothers—
not as threats or alien to others.

Freedom elevates the whole human race
beyond divisions of scorn and disgrace.
Freedom composes songs of liberty
In search of the dream of equality.

Freedom creates a new supremacy
Protected by God's superiority.
Freedom builds a nation destined to be great
By making each person the pride of the state.

For Children Safe and Strong
(Dedicated to the Children's Defense Fund)

We shall overcome has got to be more than a freedom song.
It's joining hands—across the land—for children safe and strong.
We shall overcome has got to be more than a fervent prayer.
It's sacrifice—at any price—to show them that we care.
We shall overcome has got to be more than a memory.
It's a new resolve—to get involved—in building community.
We shall overcome has got to be more than a distant dream.
It's housing, health, and jobs right now, and a place on the freedom team.

We shall overcome has got to be more than a protest song.
It's a loving vow—to learn somehow—we all can get along.
We shall overcome has got to be more than a rescue plan.

It's a wake-up call—to one and all—it's time to hope again.

We shall overcome has got to be more than a joyful sound.
It's the nation's wealth—our children's health—we cannot let them down.
We shall overcome has got to be more than a state of mind.
It's trusting God—and working hard—to leave no child behind.

Refrain
Oh—Oh—Oh.
There's a place for everyone.
Let us face the rising sun.
Then we shall overcome.

We Have Come This Far by the Power of Prayer

We have come this far by the power of prayer.
When we call on God's name, help is always there.
As we work for peace and justice, God will surely make a way.

We'll reach the Promised Land if we pray every day.

On Monday, pray . . . "Holy is Your Name.
As it is in heaven, may the earth be the same."

On Tuesday, pray . . . "Thy will be done.
May we share our bread with everyone."

On Wednesday, pray . . . "Forgive every debt.
When offended by others, forgive and forget."

On Thursday, pray . . . "Drive temptations away.
Guide us in the things we ought to do and say."

On Friday, pray . . . "Show us how to love.
Fill us with the Spirit which comes from above."

On Saturday, pray . . . "Give us Sabbath rest.
Renew and refresh us to do our best."

On Sunday, pray . . . "When we gather for
   worship and praise
with our hands lifted high this chorus
   we refrain:

(Refrain)
For Thine is the kingdom
And the power
And the glory
Forever and ever, Amen."

If You Believe My Word

If you believe My Word, step out on it,
Go forth with courage each and every day.
You will conquer doubt and apprehension
And I continue to open up the way.

When I sent Abram to an unknown land
He took a path that his feet had not trod.
By pressing his way at the Lord's command
He earned the name—a faithful friend
   of God.

When Elijah declared a coming drought
Soon the rain stopped and the rivers ceased
   to flow

He spoke to King Ahab without a doubt
If God says, "Let it be," it shall be so.

Mary was startled at the Angel's word:
"You shall bring forth God's most Holy Son"
She believed the prophecy she had heard
And brought forth Messiah—the
    Promised One.

Trust in My Word, you will find it is true
When by my utterance, your spirit is stirred.
Whatever I promise to do in you
Shall come to pass according to My Word.

GROWING UP IN the segregated South sent me north.

Most of my siblings went to Shaw University where Daddy went, starting with the eldest, Evangeline, who then trained at Columbia Teacher's College in New York and later taught at both City College and Bank Street School for Children in New York. Evangeline was quite an accomplished instructor in early childhood education. We are service-oriented people. My younger brother David went to Shaw University while the Civil Rights Movement was in full swing and was an organizer of the sit-ins at Woolworth's department store where we Blacks had not been allowed to eat at the public lunch counter. The old Woolworth was right up the street, and whenever we went by there, we always had to get our meal at the window at the end of the counter.

I remember going to buy my first meal where I could sit at the counter after the protesters were brutalized but eventually won this right after successful sit-ins. When I came into the store and sat down, a white woman who had just received her meal immediately—upon my sitting down—got up and ran out of the store. And I cannot tell you now whether I ever put in my order. But I can tell you this: I got up and went back home to South Bloodworth Street and wrote a poem called, *Thoughts at a Desegregated Lunch Counter.*

Of course, I had spent the time asking why, why can't I eat at the Woolworth [F. W. Woolworth Company] lunch counter? I grew up with the famous saying among us Blacks that all those years you walked by, you smelled the food, and if you wanted anything, you were gonna buy it at the window outside 'cause you're not gonna sit down at that lunch counter.

I remember the day when I finally was able to eat my first meal at the Woolworth counter and it was because my brother David was the president of the student body at Shaw University and had led the sit-in movement. Also David was there when the Student Nonviolent Coordinating Committee (SNCC) was born. He worked with Dr. King. David got his degree in education, became a teacher, eventually a principal in North Carolina, and for a couple of years, served as the interim dean of the school of religion at Shaw University.

Not everyone in the family went to Shaw, though. Just when you thought Shaw University was the key, there were others in our family who went the other way. Effie did her work at Morgan State. The next sister Anna also went to Morgan State and then to Howard Law School, after I had chosen Howard rather than Shaw.

Imagine a World

Where we are all free
From the ravages of hatred and bigotry
Where each newborn baby has an equal
 chance
To be nourished and to flourish and to sing
 and dance
A world where all colors know their
 common source
The bright, white light where truth is its
 force
And the rich dark soil of soul vitality
Oh, for a world where we all are free to
 live in liberty.

WHEN IT WAS time for me to decide where to go to college, I chose Howard University in Washington, DC. It was an easy choice. I was number one in my high school class—George Washington High School. I had a crush on my chemistry teacher, Susie Vick Perry. She happened to be the wife of our family doctor, Nelson Perry. In my youthful delusions, I figured that if she liked doctors, and I wanted a wife like her, then I ought to be a doctor. I decided, "I'm gonna be a doctor." In my day—graduating from high school in 1953—the chances of that were greater if you choose either Meharry or Howard. Howard had a little more appeal because it's north. I didn't want to go further south; Meharry is in Nashville. I wanted to go to Howard to do pre-med, then go to med school and fulfill my aspiration to get a wife like Susie Perry. That's why I went to George Washington High School. A crush can lead you to many things.

I started Howard in the fall of 1953, a tumultuous time in our country. I was heading north, although it's still the South. It was north of where I lived. Even though I grew up in a Black community, I remember there being a difference when I went to Howard, thinking Howard was the United Nations of Black people. Howard was a place where blackness was highlighted as the mark of excellence and the promise of the future. We had leaders from all around the world, lots of Africans, Caribbean brothers and sisters, people from all over, but you got the impression at Howard that the greatest secret in the world is what Black people will do when they finally have the opportunity to cultivate their gifts to their fullest, and that we were on the way to doing that. That's the school I went to!

At Howard, I sang at Rankin Chapel every Sunday morning under Dean Warner Lawson. I also sang under him with the National Symphony Orchestra and the Baltimore Symphony Orchestra.

While at Howard, I became a frat man, a chaplain of the Alphas [Alpha Phi Alpha Fraternity]. At Kittrell Hall they'd have Friday night dances. I absolutely loved the Friday night dances up at Kittrell Hall.

I cannot understand how I organized a study group just before the exam in one of my humanities courses. At the end of Douglas Hall is a room where I invited people to come to discuss the various authors that we read. I led those discussions. There's no reason why I—a chemistry major—should have been leading seminars in humanities as a warm-up to cram for the exam. But I was always interested in ideas, too.

I had some interesting experiences. Number one, I lived in Cook Hall and just enjoyed the fellowship there. I got a job waiting tables at Baldwin Hall. Understand this: Howard University not only had brains but the prettiest girls as well, they said, because they were hoping to snag a doctor. When you walked through Baldwin Hall Cafeteria, you thought, "God give me grace to be able to land one of these!" I recall working there, and I learned something there in Baldwin Hall. My friends and I would talk. I'm a good talker. Always, I could talk. I had the best talk, but my buddies always walked out with the prettiest girls. I learned that some things you can't talk up. I eventually became the head waiter in Baldwin Hall. As I waited tables, Dr. Martin Luther King, Jr. came to Howard University. I served him. I was honored.

The 1955 Montgomery bus boycott was the beginning of his role in promoting the movement for justice in America. He was quickly invited to speak at Howard. It was one of the first places he went as his fame began to rise across the land, and abroad. I did not become part of his coalition because at that point I was still down in the valley trying to get that chemistry taken care of. But as a waiter I had a chance to be in his company. I was so impressed by him that in 1956 my mother took me with her to hear Dr. Martin Luther King at the Needham Broughton High School in Raleigh. As a result of how I responded to him, my mother told me she knew he was going to be an important person. At the end of that same year, in 1956, after having been with Dr. King, I shifted from medicine to ministry.

I don't know whether it was that connection, but I got my call to ministry in 1956, the same year that I had been taken to hear Dr. King. Something was going on.

A Hint of Freedom

> There's a hint of freedom stirring around
>   in my soul,
> A gentle hint of freedom whispering peace.
> But freedom can't remain a hint for long—
> It has to break out as a freedom song.
> I'll tell my soul to take courage
> And to sing out strong.
>
> Woke up this morning with my mind
>   stayed on freedom
> Woke up this morning with my mind
>   stayed on freedom
> Woke up this morning with my mind
>   stayed on freedom
> Hallelu Hallelu Hallelujah!

There are bells a-ringing, calling all to be
 free.
Freedom bells are ringing, calling you and
 calling me.
When freedom calls the roll, and your
 name rings clear
Rise up, throw off the shackles of fear.
Hint no longer. Sing out strong.
Sweet freedom!

Oh, freedom, oh freedom, oh freedom
 over me
And, before I'd be a slave, I'll be buried in
 my grave
And go home to my Lord and be free.

There's a freedom tower rising, pointing
 eyes to the sky
Majestic towers rising, to tell the world why
Our heroes lived and died for the land
 that's free
Promising with pride that it shall ever be
A nation strong, secure and just in liberty.

We're free, we're free, Hallelujah!
We're free, we're free, Hallelujah, we're free.

I had a dramatic call to ministry in 1956 while I was still at Howard.

You've Got to Stop Running

> You've got to stop running
> You've got to take a stand
> If you ever hope to be
> God's preacher man.
>
> You've got to stop evading
> You've got to face the fight
> If you ever plan to serve
> The cause that's right.
>
> You've got to stop pretending
> You've got to come out real
> If you ever want to see
> Your life fulfilled.
>
> So slow down self.
> Stop and look around
> Make your best choice
> Put your best foot down.
>
> Release the strength
> You've stored up inside

Select your destination
Take a freedom ride.

So look out world
I've made up my mind
To live the truth
To seek and to find
The way of life
I've been dreaming of
The way of peace and the way of love.

When I teach homiletics, I advise my students that it is not necessary to have a dramatic calling to the ministry, but my calling defies the advice to my students because it was a most dramatic calling. It happened while I was wrestling with the issue of what my final decision should be regarding my life's vocation. During that time, I was working at the Francis Scott Key Hotel near the White House. While I was working as a bellhop there was a gentleman who would come in every night. I would take him up to his floor and as he got off the elevator, he would turn and say to me, "Young man, the Lord has a purpose for your life." Every night he came up, that's exactly what he said to me. One Friday night I went to a revival service at 1015 D St. NE near the capital. The evangelist for the revival was Reverend Equilla Lawson. That night he preached from Isaiah's call to ministry. At one point Isaiah said, "Woe is me for I am undone." Reverend Lawson said, "There are people who are in the oven but who are not yet done." I thought the preacher was talking directly to me. I knew that I was in the oven of vocational decision, and I was not done yet. I did not like the sermon. I lied when I told the minister that I enjoyed it. It disturbed me deeply. That night I went home and put on my music, which was Tchaikovsky's Symphony No. 4 in F minor. I played the music and I thought I heard in the music the part that says, "dot, dot, dot, dot, dah, dah, dah, dah, dah. . . ." I thought it was saying, "Jim Forbes, don't you know I have called you, Jim Forbes don't you know I have called you?" I was very clear that God had used Tchaikovsky and Eugene Ormandy in his Philadelphia Symphony Orchestra to call me to ministry. Then the Lord led me to read Psalms 27. Then I was urged to quote it from memory. I was amazed that I was able to quote Psalms 27, almost from memory. I was convinced surely God is calling me and this psalm would have a very important part to play in the unfolding of my ministry. Now that's a dramatic call! For sixty-eight years it has continued to hold me to the commitment I made that night.

If you are called to be a preacher and you say yes, it's because you believe that life has implored you to be a person who keeps your eye on the Lord, listens to God's guidance and then transmits that wisdom, as best you can, to the people you relate to. I've attempted to listen to the voice of the Lord in my spirit—I don't mean hallucinations or anything like that. Lord, you tell me what to do and say, and I'll do my best to convey your guidance to the people. That has been my life. My prayer every morning is:

> Holy Spirit, lead me, guide me as I move
> throughout the day.
> May your promptings deep inside me
> show me what to do and say.
> In the power of your presence, strength
> and courage will increase.
> In the wisdom of your guidance is the
> path to peace.

I've been trying to get my orders for each day since 1956.

Determined to Be Good Soil

> Lord, I have chosen to be your servant
> Forever faithful and forever true.
> Determined to be good soil for growing
> Seeds of your kingdom that are breaking
> through.
>
> The prophets and Your Son sowed seeds
> of truth

To produce love and justice everywhere.
You nurtured and watered them
    constantly
To fill the earth with signs of your care.

Forces of evil will not deter us.
Neither hate, nor greed, nor lust for power
Will recruit us for demonic measures
To block your plans for this sacred hour.

I surrender my body, soul and mind
I yield my life to the Spirit's control.
I'll help build the beloved community
To make humanity more just and whole.

Now you await a bountiful harvest
Where all dwell as neighbors in harmony.
Where righteousness flows like mighty
    streams
And the good fruit grows more abundantly.

Chorus
Love and joy, peace and patience
Springing from the tree of life
Goodness, kindness, faithfulness
Overcoming fear and strife

Gentleness and self-control
Holy signs of your kingdom
Growing daily in my soul

I'll Do Whatever You Want Me to Do

Mary was startled when the angel said,

"I have a message for you from Above.
You have been chosen
As the favored one to deliver God's
    precious gift of Love.
A wonderful child shall be born to you—
a marvelous mystery miracle birth.
If you only believe, you will receive
the most magnificent Blessing on earth."

Mary was perplexed. She just had to ask . . .

"How can this be, a peasant girl like me?
    To be chosen for such
an awesome task? Being the mother of
    Divine mystery?"

The angel answered,

"Do not be afraid. Believe in God's word,
And it shall be done.
The Spirit declares that you shall bring
    forth a little baby boy
God's Holy Son."

(and then Mary said)

"I am willing to answer your call.
Take my life and use me. I surrender all.
I will be your chosen vessel, consecrated,
    faithful and true.
Overshadow me with your spirit, Lord.
I will do whatever you want me to do."

Mary said, "Yes" to God's blessed command.
Now, she is honored all around the world.
Her story reveals that God has a plan
For every man and woman, boy and girl.
All who surrender and open their hearts
Will be blessed with heaven's spiritual birth.
That is the way the new creation starts
Spreading peace and joy all over the earth.

Chorus

Divine

If You say "Sing," I'll sing
If You say "Shout," I'll shout
If You say "Pray," I'll pray
Or testify, I'll speak out
If You say "Teach," I'll teach your word
If You say "Preach," the truth will be heard
Overshadow me with Your Spirit, Lord, and
I will do whatever you want me to do.

I FINISHED HOWARD with my chemistry degree—a bachelor of science in chemistry. I was a chemistry major who also dabbled in physics when I learned about how we have a microscopic formula of who we are—our DNA. I exhilarated in how God made a microchip of our genetic unfolding. I was ecstatic enough to write a poem thanking God for putting together a formula that was going to unfold into the ultimate expression of whom I was becoming.

Thank You for My D-N-A

> I may not be Exhibit "A" of what a saint
>   is supposed to be.
> I may not know the finer points of the
>   latest theology.
> I may not be a paragon of Christian
>   humility.

And every now and then, it's an awful sin,
How I stoop to hypocrisy.

Dear Lord, I hope you'll hear my prayer. I
confess my iniquity.
Then let me say how proud I am of my
wonderful destiny.
I celebrate what you create. I affirm all
I'm meant to be.
Thank God for the gift of life in the form
of a person like me.

Thank you for my DNA. Yes, thank you
for my DNA.
It took an artist Divine,
To make this design,
And fashion it all the way.

Thank you for my DNA. Yes, thank you
for my DNA.
You gave the design,
Now, I'm making it mine.
Thank you for my D-N-A.

But even then, I knew I was not going to continue toward medicine. I knew. In fact, the only benefit I got from my chemistry degree was I taught science at Kittrell Junior

College the year after I graduated. About all I did with that chemistry degree was teach science in Kittrell, North Carolina, before applying to Duke University to go to divinity school at Duke in Durham. Duke University wrote me a letter back saying, "We do not accept colored students, nor do we plan to do so in the foreseeable future."

Don't worry. I got a chance to preach at Duke University at the Founder's Day years later. The title of my sermon was "Let's Forgive our Fathers," and I mentioned this experience. Today I am a visiting professor at Duke University.

Drop the Thought of Dropping Out

Drop the thought of dropping out
You can make it, drop that doubt
The Lord has better plans for you
The Spirit is there to see you through

Take a deep breath and say out loud
"I don't belong in the losing crowd"
Victory is ordering the steps of my soul
I can't afford to quit until I reach my goal

With the Spirit lifting up my heart
No reason in the world to fall apart

> Overcoming power is beginning to flow
> I'm not leaving this world until it's time
> to go

I have a profound sense of God's providential care for me. Obviously, I've had my ups and downs, but I'd like to share with everybody how in a particular season of intense struggle, God—out of nowhere—made a way.

A Way Was Made

> All through the night my mind was much troubled,
> About worries awaiting the break of day.
> I tried to think of the path I could take,
> To make these heavy burdens drift away.
>
> I could not see how or what held a clue.
> No mysterious plan was close at hand.
> The Lord must have heard my state of mind,
> And whispered, "you will find a safe place to land."
>
> As I tossed on my bed, God gently said,
> "Your Provider sees what you cannot see.
> Get up, get out, go on as I guide you
> Patiently follow with your eyes on Me."

I pressed my way through routines of the
 day.
I cannot explain how the path was laid.
What prompted certain doors to open
 and close,
I kept walking with God as my aide.

When I looked around, this is what I
 found.
In Divine silence, gloom and doom began
 to fade.
Without fanfare, bright lights or flashing
 signs.
Out of nowhere, my path was now clear:
 a way was made.

AFTER ONE YEAR at Kittrell, I left. The next year I came to New York to Union Theological Seminary. I had a dramatic call to ministry in 1956, but it was not until 1958 that I started at Union Seminary.

When I left to go to seminary in 1958, my mother put two books in my suitcase. One was *Stride Toward Freedom: The Montgomery Story* by Dr. King. She knew that he had me, that something happened that night I heard him speak that had something to do with my choice to go into the ministry.

While I was packing my suitcase for my journey to Union Theological Seminary, the second book my mother placed in my bag alongside the first book was the *King James Version* of the Bible. The reason for the KJV Bible was my mother's anxiety about my studying at a liberal institution where they were probably using the RSV—the *Revised Standard Version* of the Bible, which some of my Pentecostal brothers and sisters referred to as the "Reversed Vision Bible."

The second book was given to me because my mother saw how deeply moved I was as I listened to Dr. King, as he spoke that night in 1955 when she had taken me to hear a speech by the great leader from Montgomery, Alabama. She saw that something powerful transpired in me that night, and she trusted that his book would lead me in the right direction.

On the Greyhound bus to New York City, I read that book. On the bottom of page 105 began a sentence that surprised this young holiness student on his way to seminary. That sentence said, "The Holy Spirit is the continuing community creating reality that moves through history."[1]

What! A Baptist preacher attributing to the Holy Spirit such power. Then the next sentence said, "He who works against community is working against the whole of creation." He had captured my attention and also my heart with his message.

Those affirmations were found in the chapter on "Pilgrimage to Nonviolence." Dr. King began a brief discussion of some basic aspects of the philosophy of nonviolence.

Dr. King's message comforted me on that Greyhound bus from North Carolina. I was immersed in profound

---

1 King, Martin Luther, "Pilgrimage to Nonviolence," *Stride Toward Freedom* (London: Souvenir Press, 2011), 85–86, 105.

contemplation on that ride from Duke University Divinity School. Dr. King's words were agape as I traveled to New York City to begin my training in ministry. King made sure I knew that love was the source of hope in troubled times. I read it in my sacred place of meditation. After I read about God's agape love, I understood why God's love is the greatest hope for our civilization. God's love is so powerful that it can make the unbearable bearable, the impossible possible, and transform the evils of the world to help build the beloved community.

We Are One in Your Spirit

> We are one in Your Spirit. We are one in
>   Your Love.
> Deep within, all around—below and above.
> There's no one anywhere that's excluded
>   from your care.
> Thy will, Thy will be done.
>
> One in Your Spirit. One in Your Love.
> Every tribe and nation—all from one blood.
> Created to glorify one holy name.
> God of one universe. You love us all the same.
>
> One God. One Family.
> Created in Your image—one humanity.

Everyone for justice, living abundantly.
Everybody happy, everybody free.

On the Way to Freedom

A strange thing happened on the way to freedom.
A strange thing happened on the way to justice.
A strange thing happened on the way to democracy.
I saw folks in chains who thought they'd been set free.

Some folks are still bound in ignorance.
Some folks are still bound in arrogance.
Some folks are still bound in prejudice.
They say they're free, but their chains are plain to see.

Others are still bound in hatred.
Others are still bound in bigotry.
Others are still bound in selfishness.
They need a lot of help for a strange kind of poverty.

A strange thing happened on the way to freedom.

A strange thing happened on the way to
   justice.
A strange thing happened on the way to
   democracy.
People talking about freedom found out
   they weren't quite free.

I saw Blacks and whites get together.
I saw rich and poor sharing power.
I saw gay and straight march for justice.
Both men and women singing we shall
   be free!

Let's all seek our freedom together.
Let's all break our chains together.
Let's all build a new world together.
Where peace and freedom and justice
   won't be strange.

A strange thing happened on the way to
   freedom.
A strange thing happened on the way to
   justice.
A strange thing happened on the way to
   democracy.
I saw a new community, working hard for
   equality.

ENTERING UNION THEOLOGICAL Seminary in New York City meant at that time that I was entering the best divinity school in the country. This institution of spiritual learning was ranked at the top of the list in the pantheon of other divinity schools.

My father used to come to the minister's conference at Union Theological Seminary every summer, so I had the distinction of knowing that my father was acquainted with the seminary that I would be attending. The book *Religious Affections (The Works of Jonathan Edwards)*, edited by John E. Smith, was being prepared by the editor, and my father had the chance to be in the class as he discussed some of the early work. So my daddy liked Union. He thought it was a wonderful place. He was a Pentecostal preacher but so precocious for his time. He was a progressive Pentecostal. The fact that he had come here, had sampled it, made it very special.

Spirituality

Pondering spirituality . . .
I mean to include all there is of me.
My body, mind, spirit, and emotions
Both public worship and private
    devotions
My values and habits, hopes and desires
What makes me strong and what inspires.

I think of the powers I cannot see
And how they help shape my destiny.
I think of what brings me joy and peace
When burdened, bewildered, what gives
    me release.
I think of my place in my family
And the spirit that builds up my
    community.

And I wonder if the earth is glad I'm here?
Am I spreading love or stirring up fear?
I try to discern if there's more for me.
Right here where I am or beyond the sea.
When I'm in the Spirit, these words come
    through.
"You are so precious, I'm glad I made
    you."

Holy Spirit, Lead Me, Guide Me

Holy Spirit, lead me, guide me
As I move throughout the day,
May Your prompting deep inside me
Show me what to do and say.

In the power of Your presence
Strength and courage will increase
In the wisdom of Your guidance
Is the path that leads to peace

The Fruit of the Spirit Is
(Galatians 5:22–23)

The Fruit of the Spirit is . . .
    Love, Joy, Peace
    Long-suffering, Gentleness and
        Goodness
    Faith, Meekness, and Temperance

Now that's what the Spirit produces in us.

The Fruit of the Spirit is . . .
    Love, Joy, Peace
    Even Patience, Kindness, and Generosity
    Faithfulness, Gentleness, and Self-control

Now that's what the Fruit of Spirit is.

Holy Spirit, Holy Spirit
Never cease to flow through me
May the Fruit of Your Spirit
Overflow abundantly

As long as I live
Let this my legacy be
The beautiful Fruit of the Spirit
Produced each day in me.

Union was very special because Henry Pitney Van Dusen, the president, had just written an article about Pentecostalism as the third force in Christendom. It appeared in *Life* magazine, a front-page article. When I came here, from the Black Pentecostal church, I felt quite special because I represented what Van Dusen had just been writing about. People were very interested in Pentecostalism. "What is this Pentecostalism like? Tell us about that movement," they would say. At a certain point, I thought maybe I should be the student adviser to tell people about this wonderful religious movement spreading in Latin America, and also growing in the United States.

At Union Seminary, diversity was intentional. It was considered that diversity enriches your education. Exposure to different perspectives allowed you to test out your theses, your theological perspectives, against others. So I did not feel any stigma occasioned by my Pentecostal background. Reinhold Niebuhr, one of the head theologians there, said, "You know, Jim, I hope you Pentecostals won't do as happened to the Methodists. At first, they were on fire, then they went to theological training and they lost their fire. They still have liturgy, many words, but they've lost their fire. I hope that won't happen to you. We hope that you'll keep what you have brought. Learn from others, but bring the richness that you have."

A Message of Quantum Love from God

I am usually hidden in the deep recesses
    of anonymity,
In the invisible corners of my infinity.
But sometimes the fierce urgency of
    impending calamity
Prompts my love to manifest
    extraordinary intentionality.

I see, hear, and feel groanings almost
    everywhere
Crying, Lord, have mercy! The world is
    sinking into hopeless despair.

We are obsessed with selfishness, greed,
    power, control, and tyranny.
Have we lost our senses or possibly our
    humanity?

The absence of character and decent
    values bespeak spiritual death.
The desperate plea for intervention is a
    cry for normal health.
The demise of civilization shouldn't come
    as a mystery
If trust in the divine is becoming almost
    history.

That's why I must come out of hiding to
    make myself known
Before human awareness of its sacred
    destiny is completely gone.
I must remind the nations of what, in
    creation, I was dreaming of—
A mutually affirming family held together
    by the power of my love!

Hear my call, one and all—"rise above
    hatred and fear."
All races and religions must make my
    image clear.

> The Spirit, you and I will be a Holy Trinity
> Building together the blessed beloved
> community.

Union was a place where you felt free to bring your gifts. Like we had at Howard, we recognized that just about everybody was a valedictorian, so you knew you were with some smart people, but because you were there, you also knew you could play the game.

To decide whether you had to take a first introductory course on the Bible, there was what we called the baby Bible exam. If you didn't pass the baby Bible exam, you had to take Introduction to the Bible, or a course like that. I passed the exam because I came out of a church tradition where we *knew* our Bible. Bible knowledge was a distinction by itself.

It was a very special time at Union. We were on the cutting edge of the Civil Rights Movement. We would gather students together and go down South. Even after I graduated, I remember Roger Shinn, one of my professors, joined me in Wilmington, North Carolina, where I had become a pastor. We were at sit-ins together. Social justice commitment, respect for diversity and difference, and refusal to assume that your insights will be based on whatever label you brought with you: that was Union.

Union informed my platform as a minister in two important ways. Union gave me ammunition to fight a major battle that I had as a Pentecostal. Here is the battle: in the Pentecostal tradition, if you did not speak in tongues, it was not clear that you had the Holy Spirit. And having the Holy Spirit was key. You got to have the spirit to be a preacher! Gotta have the Spirit. If you gonna be a pastor, you got to have the Spirit. But nobody ever heard me speak in tongues, and therefore, people in my tradition questioned, Can he be an authentic minister? Union taught us to be critical of the dogmas of the doctrinal verities of our tradition.

So many people approach spirituality with so many different notions that I thought it would be helpful for me to stop here and clarify. There are many understandings of spirituality. Many are very narrow. My understanding is very broad. Perhaps this poem will capture the comprehensive essence of what I believe spirituality is.

The Courage to Be Who We Are

> We need courage to be who we are
> Strength and courage to be who we are
> When trouble assails us
> And confidence fails us
> We need courage to take a stand
>
> There's no need to search for an island
> Where everybody loves your name

For as soon as you've found it
You'll soon be surrounded
By someone playing the same old game

So, I've come to this blessed conclusion
That no matter where I am
I can be fully me, courageous and free
When I remember Whose I am.

Union was helpful in giving me opportunities to broaden my exposure to other traditions and learn to appreciate other traditions. I did my field work at Church of the Master, a Presbyterian church, down the hill from Union Seminary. James Herman Robinson was pastor of that church and Dr. Eugene Callender was the associate under James, and then he became the head. James H. Robinson and I went to Operations Crossroads Africa, which was a program engaging college students in building bridges of relationships with African communities. I went with Callender, a wonderful man, to Rikers Island early Sunday mornings for services for prisoners. I remember looking out at a sea of inmates when I was called upon to read the prayer of general confession. Can you imagine! "Oh Lord, you know, here search me and know me, you know my down seats and my up rises, you know there's no good in us, spare thou those oh Lord who confess their faults, restore us oh God." The prayer of confession. Here I am with these guys confessing sins. How are they hearing this? I wondered. How am I praying it? Am I praying it for them or am I praying it for myself? It was a very, very fascinating experience to minister early Sunday mornings with Eugene Callender with Rikers Islanders as members of my congregation. While at Union, I learned that essentially your outreach was in doing internships.

I did Panel of Americans while I was at Union. That meant one Protestant, one Catholic, one Jew, and one Puerto Rican (one of whom was a woman) would go around speaking about what it means to be one community. I'm Black, I talk about my experience. This one's Latino, this one's Jewish. I developed relationships after which I was never able again to feel that God put all of God's eggs into one basket—not even my basket. I learned that God's grasp of our possibilities was so much more expansive than we could imagine. That's a radical thought for a Pentecostal preacher. I'm so delighted that I learned that if you're gonna be with God, you got to be with some strange bedfellows.

How Can You?

> How can you hate my other children
> And still expect to enjoy my grace?
> Do you fear I'll love you any less
> If I share love in another place?

> I love Jews, Christians, and Muslims, too—
> There's enough of me to love you all.
> If the wideness of my love is a problem
>   for you,
> You must have had a terrible fall.
>
> Never claim to hate in my name.
> Zeal that kills wins no prize.
> Show me your love by finding a way,
> To see all people through my eyes.

The morning after President Donald Trump referred to Haiti and South Africa as S@#$ hole nations, I was awakened by the spirit of Martin Luther King Jr. I was told that God wanted me to address the disgraceful blasphemous comments from the Oval Office. I got up and began to write a poem which I entitled, "The Divine Reprimand." When I had completed the poem, it seemed too condemnatory to send to the president. I was too intimidated about what harm would come to me and my family from president Trump or members of his base. That was in 2018, six years ago.

When the former president recently made comments about Haitians in Springfield, Ohio, destroying and eating the pets of the citizens of that community, I was reprimanded with these words of judgment; if you had delivered words to president Trump back in 2018, perhaps we may have avoided much of the death and destruction of recent years.

I then became aware of the truth that many of us deserve God's reprimand for our transgressions, if we had been obedient to the Divine will, our nation could have avoided the plagues of multiple polarizations and oppressions. During this election year it is my prayer that we will not only condemn Trump for his innumerable crimes and iniquities but that each of us will do our best to discern God's will and to do what the creator God would have us to do.

The Divine Reprimand
(to those who refer to others in degrading
and disrespectful terms)
Sacred **H**umanity **I**n **T**ransformation

Don't ever call people that again.
Whatever their flaws, they are precious
to ME.
Though marred and scarred and incomplete,
In My hands, I am shaping their destiny.

Many and varied are the imperfections,
Of all finite souls who walk the Earth.
My Love is a lab for their refinement,
Tweaking the design before and after birth.

I am the Potter, you are the clay.
I honor your freedom to be who you may.
I assure you, I will lure you constantly.
To be the kind of person you were meant
    to be.

Persist and resist, yet I will insist.
Recalibrating our choreography.
In the tension of your struggle, my
    tenacious love
Will steadily prod you below and above.

What you called odious waste,
Excrement, trash, slop for swine.
In time, they will be seen for the treasures
    they are:
A rare work of art by an Artist Divine.

In the midst of the muddle and smelly mess.
As I work against evasion, denial and delay.
With patience, I'll wait to seize the
    moment of grace,
To show you My own image in every
    human face.

Narcissism sees and makes itself divine.
Defacing in others, the likeness of Mine.

Such blasphemous debasement demeans every race,
Nothing casts out such demons, but My saving grace.

There is no superior nation, tribe or class.
Self-assigned supremacy is a malignant mass.
Learn to build together—no walls of separation,
All are Sacred Humanity in Transformation.

Now that we see how white supremacy
In creating slaves disfigured the free.
Imagine how beautiful life will be
Healed from the scars of racial bigotry.

Our dear nation needs an emancipation,
From racialistic incarceration.
Truth gladly offers forgiveness and grace
In exchange for the myths built upon race.

Choosing justice may feel like suicide—
Releasing power, privilege, and pride.
An extremely costly sacrifice,
but for peace of mind, A MODEST PRICE.

Now that we see how white supremacy
In creating slaves disfigured the free,
Imagine how beautiful life will be
Healed from the scars of racial bigotry.

Our dear nation needs an emancipation
From racialistic incarceration.
Truth gladly offers forgiveness and grace
In exchange for the myths built upon race.

Choosing justice may feel like suicide
Releasing Power, Privilege, and Pride.
An extremely costly sacrifice,
but for peace of mind, A MODEST
    PRICE.

Without fabrication, the human race is a
    masterpiece,
we must not deface.

Sisters and Brothers,
Let us dare to be

Beloved Community,
one family.

DURING MY YEARS of training for ministry, I began to see what was at work in the hearts and minds of those who were locked into prejudice and bigotry. I searched for a better understanding of what racism does to whites as well as Blacks. I was desperate to discover if there was anything in my faith tradition strong enough to deliver our people from the grip of the demon-possession of racism. I spent many years searching for what would deliver us all from this congenital defect in our national psyche.

At the end of my second year as a student at Union Theological Seminary in New York City, I decided to take a year off to do an internship with my father, Bishop James A. Forbes Sr. He was serving as pastor of Providence Holy Church in Raleigh, North Carolina, my hometown. I interrupted my ministerial training to get some sense of what it would be like to serve as a minister in a southern Pentecostal congregation after being trained at the predominantly white, liberal Union Seminary. What

I learned during that year reassured me that, although I was leaning toward a more progressive approach to the ministry, I could make a valuable contribution to the church of my youth. I felt a profound sense of gratitude for the role it had played in helping to shape my character and religious sensibilities. Some years later, one of my role models, Carlisle Marney, a white Southern Baptist minister, confirmed the wisdom of my choice. He said, "Jim, no man ever amounts to much until he learns to bless his own origins."

During that intern year on January 11, 1961, I had an experience I wrestled with throughout the next forty-seven years of my life. That day was the first time I was able to sit down and order a meal at the lunch counter of the Woolworth Five and Dime department store on Fayetteville Street in Raleigh.

I was twenty-five years old and I had lived my entire youth in the segregated South. I was thoroughly familiar with the etiquette and protocols of the Jim Crow Society: separation of Black and white was the norm. I had experienced colored water fountains, colored restrooms, colored neighborhoods, colored schools, and colored churches—even colored hospitals and cemeteries. I knew the place assigned to me and my brothers and sisters of African descent.

In 1957, I had been reminded of the inevitable but palpable line. I had applied to Duke Divinity School in Durham, North Carolina. Their letter of rejection explained that they did not accept Negro students, nor did they expect to do so in the foreseeable future. Many years later, when I spoke on Founder's Day at Duke University Chapel, I reminded the community of the letter I had received. My sermon that day was titled "Let's Forgive Our Fathers."

Things had begun to change only a few years after that Duke rejection. In 1960, beginning with sit-ins at a lunch counter in Greensboro, North Carolina, students from A&T (Agricultural and Technical) University sparked a brushfire of civil disobedience protests. My brother David was then the student body president at Shaw University in Raleigh. He organized and led demonstrations at the local Woolworth store. After a brief struggle, the segregationist policy was dropped. At last, Blacks could sit down for a meal at the lunch counter rather than having to buy take-out lunches at a window. What a liberating moment! It symbolized the breaking of the chains of second-class citizenship. It was an answer to generations of mothers' and fathers' prayers that their sons and daughters would be respected as full human beings with all the rights and privileges of citizenship. It was Montgomery, Birmingham, and Selma—right there in my hometown. The battle for equality and justice had been fought and won. The Jericho walls were falling down everywhere, or so it seemed.

I felt a primal sense of delight as I made my way to the Woolworth store and sat down at the counter, ready to order lunch. Immediately after I sat down, the white woman sitting in the seat to my right got up and stormed out of the store! It was as if an illegal alien from another planet had invaded her sacred space. Her reaction shocked me to the core. It was such a disturbing moment that I cannot recall whether I eventually ordered the hot dog with catsup, mustard, and relish, and a big orange soda that I had anticipated consuming at the lunch counter.

My response was not simply a matter of how disturbed I was by her reaction. It was obvious that I had disturbed her deeply as well. I had been taught by my parents, church, and community not to do to others what I would not have done to me. I wondered what exposed nerve I had struck simply by making use of public services licensed to serve everybody and thereby claiming the right to be a full citizen. I wondered if she felt that I was a slightly less-human person than herself, or maybe she was afraid I intended some harm to her, or maybe her distress was greater, as if her entire world was shaken. Perhaps my presence so close to her signaled that her protective wall of whiteness had sprung a leak that would flood her safe sanctuary of exclusion.

I can't remember if I ordered a meal that day, but I remember that I went home embarrassed, humiliated, hurt, and angry. I sat down and expressed my rage in a poem that I called,

Thoughts at a Desegregated Lunch Counter

Why did she move when I sat down?
Surely, she could not tell so soon
That my Saturday bath had worn away
Or that savage passion
Had pushed me toward rape.

Perhaps it was the cash she carried in her
    purse;
She could not risk a theft so early in the
    month.
And who knew that on tomorrow would
    fall her lot
To drink her coffee from a cup
My darkened hands had clutched?

So horrible was that moment
I too should have run away
For prejudice has the odor of a dying beast.
Whether rapist or racist, both fall in the
    savage class

> And the greatest theft of all is to rob one's
> right to be.

Long after I had forgotten the poem, it was returned to me thirty years later when I was the Senior Minister of The Riverside Church in New York City, a congregation that was 60 percent white and 40 percent Black. A white parishioner had requested an appointment to meet with me. After we greeted each other, she explained the purpose of her visit: "I was going through some of my old letters when I ran across a letter that you sent me in 1961. It had this poem in it and I thought you might like to have it." It was the poem I had written after the Woolworth experience. I was startled both because she had kept it and because I wondered why I would send such an expression of pain and disappointment to a white woman living in the same southern city as the woman who occasioned such anguish in my youthful, tender heart. Two white women, living in the same city. What was the difference?

I never again saw the woman who ran from the Woolworth lunch counter. I wish I could talk to her, to understand how she had experienced the event. I was sure that it was my Black presence that had repelled her. Was it a threat or disgust she felt? What was it that made it impossible for her to finish her meal while I was sitting at the counter next to her? A conversation with her might have given me insight into the deep chasm between some members of the white and Black communities. I still regret that I never met her again or knew her name.

What I had sensed about my white parishioner when I knew her back in 1961 explains why I sent her a copy of my poem. Her name was Dorothy Marcus. At the time of the Woolworth incident, she was a student at Meredith College in Raleigh, North Carolina, and working at the United Church on Hillsborough Street. The white congregation provided educational and recreational programs for young people in the Black community. The spirit of her leadership and the genuineness of her counsel and care left me certain that what touched me deeply also mattered to her. I was sure that she would want to know what had happened to me and what could be done about it. I wanted to let her know about my fears and my anger. Her caring witness reassured me that not all people are the same, even though they are of the same racial group.

By the time Dorothy Marcus returned my poem to me three decades later, she had moved north and was an active member of The Riverside Church. She was still involved in racial-justice work, seeking to move the church and society beyond racial polarization. She championed mutual respect, multicultural affirmation, and shared aspirations. Riverside was still struggling to understand racism, its roots, the various forms of its current manifestations, and its consequences. The Social Justice Commission of the church sponsored forums and workshops to explore ways to overcome the pernicious effects of racism and to safeguard coming generations against its viral toxicity. These Church actions were a far cry from what I experienced thirty years before.

In the fall of 1961, after my intern year in Raleigh, I returned to Union Seminary. Freshly alerted to continuing racism, I signed up for a course on race taught by George Kelsey, a visiting professor from Drew University School of Theology. The principal resource for the course was his manuscript, later published as *Racism and the Christian Understanding of Man*. This course helped me probe more deeply the theological issues beneath racial prejudice, discrimination, and segregation. Kelsey explained that, for some people, race functions as a faith perspective. Racial oppression can be very strong and intractable because it operates on the level of religious commitment. The white woman who ran out of the Woolworth store was probably not aware of it, but she may have had a religiously held conviction about race! Dorothy Marcus on the other hand, was bearing witness to the principles of her faith tradition as well when she reached out with love and understanding to Blacks. Conversations about racism and the power to overcome it are more fruitful if we are aware that we are dealing with two different and opposing "gospels." There is the gospel of racial exceptionalism and the gospel of human equality of being.

Years later in 2020, in a Presbyterian Mission lecture series, I asked if participants paid attention to the fact that the statues of Confederate heroes were being pulled down and reminded participants that that may be an act just to keep us aware that hope is possible. "Change can come through deliverance not yet announced," I told them. Nevertheless, God is working all the time. And then I asked: "Did you notice the extraordinary diversity that came as a result of a response to George Floyd's murder? Did you notice the diversity there? In fact, I thought that with the murder of George Floyd, the knee on his neck by one officer and other officers on his body reminded me of a colossal elephant sitting on people of color." In this situation, the Lord reminded me—in the diversity in the people protesting, with Black communities and white communities holding signs reading "Black Lives Matter"—of that definition of racism I heard in 1962 while a student in Dr. George D. Kelsey's class at Union. Nearly sixty years later, it affected the way I responded to what happened to George Floyd. "A plague, I thought, a plague of police brutality." Kelsey defined racism as a dogma that one ethnic body is condemned by nature to hereditary inferiority and another group is destined to hereditary superiority. According to that dogma, the whole of civilization depends on eliminating some races. It is the dogma that one race alone has carried progress for human history and ensures future progress. The chief political plan of racists has been segregation, isolation, and deprivation, but despite the prevailing practices of segregation, the underlying logic of racism is genocide.

We Shall Overcome, for Sure

Supremacists, more bigoted and bold.
Leaders in high places, ruthless and cold.
Why do we keep on singing hopeful songs—
In the midst of hateful, brutal wrongs?
What keeps our hearts and minds from
    sinking down
While we're oppressed and our spirits bound?

Do we know something others do not know?
Why couldn't we give up when hate sank
    so low?
Why didn't we stop protesting while
    families grieve?
When our eyes saw evil, we couldn't believe?

Why do we still march with justice
    demands?
Chanting and singing with uplifted hands?

We sing because we know God is on the
    throne—
At work in everything, known and
    unknown.

So, we won't win the battle ev'ry day.
Faith trusts God to have the final say.
Whether we live or die, confronting wrong.
We shall overcome for sure, that's our song.

I ENJOYED UNION Theological Seminary as a place of learning. My seminary days sealed the love of God and community in my heart. Living in New York was edifying for me.

I obtained my master of divinity degree in 1962 from Union Theological Seminary, which coincidentally was across the street from The Riverside Church. I later earned my clinical pastoral education certificate from the Medical College of Virginia in Richmond and my doctorate of ministry from Colgate Rochester Crozer Divinity School. Ultimately, I feel my career started at Union Theological Seminary. I later returned and served as the Joe R. Engle Professor of Preaching from 1976 until 1985, when I moved across the street, called to pastor The Riverside Church.

After graduating from Union Theological Seminary in 1962, I was assigned as a student minister at an all-white Southern Baptist church, Olin T. Binkley Baptist

Church, in Chapel Hill, North Carolina, on the campus of the University of North Carolina. Dr. Robert Seymour made me his assistant for the entire summer. We celebrated Holy Communion as the first interracial leaders on that campus. I went back South to participate in a program called Student Interracial Ministry. Sponsored by the National Council of Churches, the program put Black pastors in white congregations and white ministers in Black ones. They decided that if we are to do anything about changing church segregation, we need to put Black preachers in white churches so people get used to them, so congregants know what that's like. It was an attempt to overcome some of the history of discrimination in churches.

I was only there for a short time. It was a difficult time for the congregants. Dr. Robert Seymour helped lead Chapel Hill to a greater openness about racial matters. He had a sense of being a part of the movement for justice and equality. Working with Dr. Seymour, I had some interesting experiences. First of all, when the deacons and I would go down the street to The Rathskeller—that's the big restaurant that people like on Franklin Street on the campus at the University of North Carolina—they would refuse to serve us. When we took our youth group out to play baseball, there would be N-word calling as I served as an umpire. I went to North Carolina Memorial Hospital to visit

Mrs. Bert Adams [Diane Adams] who had just had a baby while Dr. Seymour was on a trip. I was the pastor in charge. I went to the hospital reception and said, "Excuse me, I'm here to visit Mrs. Bert Adams." The response: "Well, this is the white maternity ward. Obviously you're looking for the one over on the other side." I said, "No, I'm here as a pastor at the Olin T. Binkley Church. I'm the interim minister there." "She can't . . . ," the receptionist trailed off. There I am, on a pastoral visit to greet Mrs. Adams and the new baby, to bless the white baby, and I thought, *My God, what is wrong with this picture from their perspective!*

Of course, there were many different situations like these. But somehow fear didn't occur to me. I don't recall times where I feared for my life. I knew that these people were faced with experiences beyond what they had known, and I felt they had a right to be apprehensive. I didn't have to join that crowd, though. I didn't have to be afraid of them like they were afraid of me. In those days you would tend to anesthetize yourself to threats. Somehow it worked both ways. As Ralph Ellison in *Invisible Man* says, they don't see me because to them I'm invisible. We also had the capacity not to see the indignity if we didn't choose to.

You know what, I'll be quite frank about this. If you grew up in the South, one of the things you remembered is that Emmett Till was brutally murdered for supposedly simply looking at a white woman, right? They said he whistled at her, or something like that. Black boys were taught *you don't* look at white women. So, one of the most anxious times for me was going with the church to the church picnic at Carolina Beach near Wilmington. At the beach, you get into your bathing gear. I was a little uncomfortable in that setting. The intimacy of community on the beach, in bathing suits, was a violation of what had been taught.

Seeing Myself Through the Eyes of God

> A woman was arrested by men of
>   righteous claim
> They said her loose behavior was an awful
>   shame
> Their judgment apparent for mere pious
>   display
> The other guilty party simply slipped away
>
> Jesus wrote down their secret sins right
>   there on the ground
> When He stood up and looked around,
>   accusers were not found
> Then Jesus spoke to her with the
>   gentleness of a dove

Leaving the woman in the hands of God's
    forgiving love

Many suffer shame of condemnation
For who they are and what they may have
    done
But Jesus feels the grief from all our failures
And cares for men and women—everyone

Just as he forgave the woman's transgressions
And urged her to go and sin no more
God's grace accepted her sincere confessions
And began to heal her soul from the core

I used to live in bondage to other people's
    whims
Who said they know who God accepts
    and also condemns
I could not possibly deserve God's love in
    their eyes
I feared my full potential could not be
    realized

So, I held myself hostage to a downgraded
    me
Stripped of self-esteem, only my failures I
    could see

I half-stepped, covered up and feigned
    what was not true
Hoping God would reveal to me what I
    ought to do

Then I heard amazing words that almost
    blew my mind
"God's love is not reserved for the
    so-called righteous kind
The grace of God is for great and small,
    fit and feeble as well
If we open our hearts, God's love is
    pleased there to dwell"

No more need for self-loathing; God cares
    where we're found
Let's embrace God's grace and start the
    race toward higher ground
We'll find strength of forgiveness and
    strive for truth each day
God, the loving Potter, will find a better
    way

Thank you, thank you, thank you, God
    above
For seeing us through the eyes of your love

Through all my struggles on the path I've trod
I see myself now through the eyes of God.

God's Dream of the World

This is the world I've been dreaming of.
This is the world I've been looking for.
A world I call a "beloved community"
Everybody valued, secure and free.

Dedicated to the common good.
Diversity welcomed in the neighborhood.
No oppression or domination.
Justice is the goal of every nation.
Love the only true supremacy.
Many ethnicities—one family.

Bigotry is condemned as evil and vile.
Warfare and sedition out of style.
Children respecting and enjoying each other.
The needy cared for as sister and brother.
The whole atmosphere as sacred space.
I and humanity in a love embrace.

Now that's the kind of world I've been
    dreaming of.

> That's the kind of world I've been
>   looking for.
> Wake up and dream along with me
> And build the kind of world I intend it
>   to be.

After the Student Interracial Ministry experience, my next appointment was pastor of Holy Trinity Church, in Wilmington, North Carolina. It sounded like an Episcopal church, but it was Pentecostal. My father was the bishop of the southern district. He combined three small Pentecostal churches into one church and named it Holy Trinity Church.

Church folk said, "Now the bishop may have given him this position, but does the boy have the Holy Ghost?" You understand me? The bishop was my daddy. Nepotism or not, fundamentally throughout my time as a developing minster in the Pentecostal tradition, the problem was: "We've never heard him speak in tongues. Could he really have the Holy Spirit?" When I went to my first large church pastorate, in the tradition, the push back was, "We never heard him speak in tongues. How can he help us get the blessing?"

At Union Seminary, I had begun what turned out to be a lifelong personal study on the Holy Spirit, what the tradition really says about signs and symbols. It's a mark of pride to say I sat through the Monday morning lectures in

October of 1959 when Paul Tillich, the world-renowned theologian, did his third volume of his systematic theology on the Holy Spirit. As I was listening, I had come to call myself a Tillichian Pentecostal, because it gave me a theological framework to understand that you can't put God in a box. I don't care what your religious tradition is, God is not going to fit neatly in the categories of your doctrinal formulations. That became my approach to Pentecostalism.

Sweet Communion

Oh, how sweet and oh how pleasant
Is communion in Your Love
Safe and secure in the presence
Of Your Spirit from above

Sweet contentment, holy quietness
Grace and mercy in Your love
Shekinah glory like a river
Flowing from Your courts above

I HAD MET Bettye Franks at Howard University. However, I did not marry Bettye until 1964 after reconnecting with her at an annual convocation of the United Church of America in Goldsboro, North Carolina. We were married a year later, while I was pastoring Holy Trinity Church in Wilmington, North Carolina.

I met Bettye singing in the Howard University choir under the direction of Dean Warner Lawson. I noticed the beautiful alto from San Antonio, Texas, and asked to be introduced to her. One of my friends introduced me to her with the mild warning: "She may be a little too swift for you." Although we sang in Rankin Chapel each Sunday morning, Bettye was also performing as a pianist in a nightclub at Seventh and T, not too far from the university. We met, shook hands, and that was the extent of our acquaintance at Howard.

Six years later after both of us had graduated from Howard and had moved to North Carolina, we met again at the Southern District Convocation of the United Holy Church of America. At the end of the worship service, when the offering was being received, different sections of the congregation were invited to bring their offerings to the front of the church. I saw Bettye as she walked back to her seat in the audience. I made my way to where she was seated and asked, "Don't I know you?" But we did not recognize each other, we didn't place each other, until the singing of the doxology. My baritone voice made me known to her. That was the moment of recognition, the moment of divine connection.

Shortly thereafter we were engaged. On Friday, June 13, 1964, we were married at the church I was pastoring, Holy Trinity Church in Wilmington, North Carolina. We became a ministry team of pastoring, teaching, and preaching, and Bettye was the musical associate. Bettye and I began our ministry there, and I served that church until I left to go to Saint John's Holy Church in Richmond, VA in 1965.

When I was called to be the Pastor at The Riverside Church in New York, Bettye founded the Ebony Ecumenical Ensemble. She had led her choir to Brazil, to South Korea, and all over the United States. She was a wonder and has continued to intrigue me ever since.

Beautiful Nappy Hair—The Miracle in the Black Hair Salon

Angels were sent to do a site visit in the Black hair salon. What is the atmosphere in such a place? What goes on in there throughout the day? The angels reported:

It is a most welcoming and affirming setting. Outer garments are hung in sight so that clients know they are safe and secure or in a closet the person may choose.

People are greeted as if they are one family, shaking hands or giving hugs to some or hello to others. They find comfortable seats or sofas or pick up magazines or take out their cell phones or tablets. Some put on headphones and tune in to their favorite music. When it is time to be served, they are appropriately cloaked so their clothes will not get wet or stained by the experience. There is usually a sequence of shampooing, conditioning, various levels of drying, hair clipping, and if necessary, some texturing oil or preparatory gel—all these to get ready for the styling process. This may require rollers, clips, hairpins, wraps, attachments, extensions, and even beads and assorted trinkets, and sometimes twisting besides. Many times, there may be styling gels or sprays to hold things in place or wraps to fix the magic until it dries as the stylist intends. Did I leave out the braiding or plaiting process, which may take one or even five to eight hours, depending upon the complexity of the design or the length or texture of the hair. While all this is going on, the beautician is listening, counseling, discussing religion, relationships, nutrition, or sharing a good joke or two. Madam C. J. Walker may be beaming down her approval from her high perch in glory.

When the process is completed, the stylist proudly holds up a mirror so they both can celebrate the artistic work of beautification that has taken place. Occasionally there is a request for minor adjustments, but generally there is a consensus that all is well that ends well.

As the clients are leaving the salon, the angels request opportunities to interview some of them about what the experience was like and how it affected the way they felt within. They all agreed that it was tiring but worth enduring the process. One client said my stylist actually became a therapist for me. Another said, my stylist is a gay man. He is the best, not only in how he styles my hair but the gentleness of his touch, and also the way he engages me in conversation. Sometimes it seems like a spiritual experience.

The most frequent comments were:

"It was uplifting!"
"It relaxed my whole body."
"It made me feel like a queen."
"It was so nourishing to my spirit."
"I felt like a precious and beloved person."
"It made me feel beautiful both inside and outside."
"It took my stress away."
"My troubled thoughts vanished."
"I felt like I owned the world."
"Was ready to take on the world!"

But this is what God told the angels about what happened in the salon: Miracles actually took place!

Black women, young girls, and even children who had been downgraded by stigmas of racist comments about their hair, bearing psychic scars from dismemberment from human family, emotionally battered and bruised by a sense of nobodiness, who had heard comments about their hair that made their eyes water with tears, who had been affected by culturally contrived aesthetics of white preference, entered the salon one way but departed having received a sense of pride in the natural endowments I had given them. Now that was a miracle! They departed the salon in a triumphant spirit, seeing themselves through the eyes of God. God looked at their styles and said, "WOW!"

But when the angels along with God observed the remarkable varieties of their beautiful angelic styles, they exclaimed together, "Glory hallelujah in the highest heavens and on the whole Earth."

At one point in the Black Liberation Movement, women found the freedom to wear their hair in its natural style. Some people—both Black and white—thought it was unbecoming; but Black women felt so emancipated, they didn't care what people said about their afros. I thought I'd write a poem to help celebrate their freedom to wear their hair any way they wanted to.

> What a beautiful sight, the nappy head
> Of brave souls recently raised from the dead.
> Death of self-loathing and self-negation
> Death of racial stigmatization.
>
> My grandmother's hair, now hoary and gray
> Brushed my brow, wiping my tears away.
> Though nappy and thinning, no longer fair
> Felt like angel's wings, the touch of her hair.
>
> Remember after a passionate night,
> You awake and take in your very first sight?
> Her hair is disheveled, all out of place.
> I've never seen such a beautiful face.

Your daughter survives a brain operation
After a most bleak prognostication.
You don't notice the texture of her hair
Because you are happy, she's still there.

Hairstyle doesn't matter, nor does its length.
What really counts is character and strength.
Appreciate the ones who just don't care
What others may think or say about your
    hair.

What a wonderful nation we could be
Encouraging our neighbors to be free.
To select and design their own profile
Even the uniqueness of their hairstyle.

What Kind of Love Are You Dreaming Of?
(My love for Bettye Franks Forbes)

What kind of love are you dreaming of?
What kind of love are you looking for?
What kind of love will really satisfy?
Let me know my love, and I'll bring it on
    by.

This is the love I've been dreaming of.
This is the love I've been looking for.
This is the love that will satisfy.
If you've got that kind of love, then bring it on by.

Thoughtful, patient, tender, and tough,
Surprising and playful, but never too rough.
Sunshine steady, wind blowing free,
Rain-drenching pleasure spreading all over me.

Makes you dream in the daytime,
Keeps you awake throughout the night.
Makes you love to give your all,
Cause this loving's "oh so right!"

And when the loving's over,
Love keeps lingering around.
Our heart holds hands in silence,
While the passion simmers down.

Now that's the kind of love I've been dreaming of.
That's the kind of love I've been looking for.

That's the kind of love that will satisfy.
If you've got that kind of love then bring
 it on by.

The Beautiful Truth About Naomi and Ruth

The beautiful truth about Naomi and Ruth,
Is they knew the meaning of love.
Not the sentimental kind, you often find,
Hollywood lovers dreaming of.

These hearts were joined in a common bond,
Yet they helped each other be free.
When the harvest turned bad, they still
 were glad,
To face life as a family.

Each had the strength of self-esteem:
They made their own decisions.
Yet both could smile, at the other's style,
And support each other's vision.

The ways they differed enriched their lives
With spark and charm and daring.
So, they strategized and improvised
Creative patterns of sharing.

Together, they walked the path of life.
God's grace took its place beside them.
Before too long, there was love so strong,
No threat or harm could divide them.

This humble tale of Naomi and Ruth,
Is a message of grace from above.
There is nothing we know, on the earth below,
That can sever us from God's love.

MY NEXT CHURCH was in Richmond, Virginia, at St. John's United Holy Church. It was a big, established church pastored by the old conservative Bishop William Clements.

During this period, the Civil Rights Movement was growing, combusting. Richmond was for me always the most tantalizing place I ever went to. It felt like justice was right around the corner but never quite there. It was a town that enjoyed tranquility and stability, but I learned at that time that it wasn't going to let Blacks get but so far. I was in Richmond as a pastor from 1965 through 1973. The Voting Rights Act of 1965 was affecting social climate, and for many in Virginia this was the first time they were able to vote. It was an interesting time. For example, there was a Republican governor, Linwood Holton, who proved to be a human being. Republicans at the time were not the Republicans of today, yes? The Dixiecrats were the die-hard racists/segregationists.

Today's stigmas on Republicans began when those Dixiecrats moved to the Republican Party as the Democratic Party liberalized. Linwood is the father of Anne Holton, wife to Senator Tim Kaine (Democrat, Virginia). Even back in the mid-1960s, I thought, Governor Holton may be Republican, but he's not in the same batch as those who are not sensitive to the need for inclusion.

During my time in Richmond, St. John's had a series of activities to help the Black community. When violence would break out, we pastors would be invited to try to figure out how to keep the community from being too restless. When a garbage dump was going to be placed in back of Armstrong High School, we protested and I paid a visit to Alan F. Kiepper (who later became the city manager of Atlanta, Georgia) and we argued about where they were going to place that garbage dump. He took us in the city planning board and, for the first time, showed us these big maps on the wall, saying, "Listen, I know you all are concerned about this problem, but you need to understand the way cities function. They have long-range plans. This is the zoning for the next twenty-five years." This taught me that we who are dealing with social issues need to be aware of the larger context in which our struggle is taking place. I learned from looking at those big maps that a manufacturing section was going to be in the residential section, where we have the schools, and highways would be developed, decimating our neighborhoods. I learned that our community needed to plan, to speak about what the community renewal program would be. "Folks, let's get sophisticated enough to speak out that we don't want that smoke blowing into the classrooms where our kids are learning," I urged. "We really have got to get involved in this process. Last-minute protest does not substitute for long-range, strategic planning." This awareness came to me in Richmond as a Pentecostal preacher.

During this time, I was also campus minister of Virginia Union University and taught at Union Presbyterian Seminary at Virginia Union. During those years in Richmond I had at least ten different jobs while I was pastor of St. John's United Holy Church, a congregation of maybe two or three hundred people.

My wife Bettye and I were newly wed, living in a house that was owned by the church, a parsonage, and Bettye taught music at John F. Kennedy High School and Armstrong High School. We learned later on that money is important, but our parents had taught us money wasn't important, that we were God's kids and God would make a way for us. We almost got too spoiled in that notion because, I'll tell you, as you retire and are on fixed income, you say the Lord needs a little help, or at least we need to help the Lord by helping ourselves.

Bettye was there at St. John's and she was the director of the church choir, one of the best choirs in town.

Eventually, I was chosen the head of the Richmond Black clergy. I also started the neighborhood Legal Aid Society and the Progress Association for Economic Development, one of Leon Sullivan's outposts. He was the founder of the Progress Association for Economic Development of Philadelphia. I served on the board of the United Giver's Fund. During that time, I served as president of the Urban League of Greater Richmond.

I earned my clinical pastoral education certificate from the Medical College of Virginia in Richmond, in 1968, the year Dr. King was assassinated. Clinical training is a program preparing ministers for chaplaincy work in hospitals and other institutions.

During my time at St. John's United Holy Church, I was aware an important book was published, *Black Theology and Black Power* by James Cone. I was fascinated when I first met Jim Cone at Howard University at a conference on theological education in 1970. The book was written in 1969. I met this young guy, this young dude, James Cone, and I was so moved by what he said!

A preacher named Henry Mitchell had written a book in 1974, *Black Preaching: The Recovery of a Powerful Art.*

I devoured their books because about this time I was a campus minister at Virginia Union. Miles Jones was pastor of Providence Park Baptist Church in Richmond and Paul Nichols was pastor of Good Shepherd Baptist Church in Richmond. We three guys shared the job of chaplaincy, and we also taught together. We started a course at Virginia Union on Black theology and preaching in the Black liberation context. We started taking Jim Cone's ideas and Henry Mitchell's ideas and training Christians to address the liberation agenda of the Black community.

I was still pastoring, and I decided in my church to wear a dashiki every so often. Maybe once a month, I wore a dashiki and used my African drum that I had brought back with me from Africa to say, *We've got to be a part of the movement, the Black is Beautiful movement.* I had a beard during that period.

I wrote a sermon during that time entitled "How to be Black and a Christian Too" because Black theology started to call into question the validity of white theology that had not addressed the condition of Black people. Jim Cone said, if you don't recognize Jesus is Black—a Palestinian Jew, dark-skinned, not this blue-eyed European we see in paintings; if your religion has not dealt with blackness, your religion is suspect. Most of us in the South are trained to be respectful and affirming of others even if we disagree with them. It required us to seriously question the authenticity of the religion we had inherited from the white community that had ignored our Black existence. Jim Cone took Jesus's blackness and made that the center. We had to figure out how to disengage from our loyalty to the religion of the enslavers and dare to believe that our own experience is the beginning of the genuine faith Jesus was invested in. It was shocking at first. Cone reversed the tables. It was a revolutionary experience.

I was serving at St. John's when Reverend Dr. Martin Luther King Jr. was assassinated. In a sense, Richmond managed to come through without the level of violence that we remember in Washington, DC, on Fourteenth Street. Richmond was spared the more incendiary aspects of protests. I remember the day Dr. King was assassinated. I was on my way to Virginia Commonwealth University School of Medicine where I was taking a chaplaincy course they called clinical pastoral education. As I was traveling across the Marshall Street Bridge, the news came. I started crying. I could hardly see for the tears in my eyes and feared that with my teary vision, I might not make it safely across. But I did. When I turned into the parking lot, I sat there with my hands on the steering wheel and said, "Martin, you shall not have died in vain." That was my commitment to make sure that what he had given his life for, I was going to be engaged in seeing it through. I recall that moment so very clearly. That's, by the way, the same bridge that was torn down and replaced by a new bridge named the Martin Luther King Jr. Memorial Bridge.

Post Dr. King's assassination, we knew that it was okay to be arrested. We participated in sit-ins. We were prepared to answer the question Alan Boesak asked: *When people ask you what happened to your scars, was there nothing worth fighting for?* It began to be a mark of genuineness to feel strongly about something enough to risk loss of well-being and even, if necessary, to lose your life.

WE MOVED WITH our baby son, James A. Forbes III, to Washington, DC, in 1973 to serve Intermet Seminary, Interfaith Metropolitan Theological Education, Inc., Washington, DC, which had only recently been founded following the 1968 riots.

John Caldwell Fletcher, an Anglican priest said, "If we're gonna manage, we're gonna learn how to live together." He said, "Why should you consider yourself trained and you don't even know what the problems are in the context of your congregation? You at least need to know what the questions are." He put together this seminary without walls, asking congregations to become the central learning places for the students. Once or twice a week we'd get together for theological reflections on what was happening. We developed Protestant, Catholic, and Jewish congregations. We had fifty or sixty congregations where students could come as student ministers. They worked for forty hours a week. You work for forty in a congregation, you know what the questions are.

We would come together for a couple of days, those majoring in the biblical field, historical field, the theological field, and the practical field. You have greater learning in each of these disciplines because you bring questions rather than just a tabula rasa. That seminary reinforced the significance of learning to be faith people together.

During this time, in the summer months and all along the way, I was working on the doctorate of ministry from Colgate Rochester Crozer Divinity School in Rochester, New York. Twenty of the most promising pastors were chosen to refine their gifts in terms of the new emphasis on Black religious experience. We were called Martin Luther King Jr. fellows. In the DMin program we would take trips together with the faculty, trips to Africa, Jamaica, Haiti, the Sea Islands of North Carolina. We were learning in the situation, and then we would go to Colgate Rochester to do our reflective and writing portions of this work. Most of the residencies were during the summer months and during the rest of the year, there was travel. This was funded by the Irving and Sweeney Miller Foundation.

Thus, Saith the Lord

I love all my children equally.
I want all my children to be free.

It grieves me when they live in constant alarm
Assaulted, abused, and victims of harm.

I urge you to join me in my daily quest,
To heal their diseases and release their best.
I won't stop working until they finally see
The world as a safe space and beloved
    community:
Neighbors living in harmony.

We All Can Be Philanthropists

All members of the human race,
Our blue-green earth is sacred space.
Let us partner with God to co-create
A world we all can celebrate.

Our daily deeds are landscape seeds.
Are we sowing thorns and toxic weeds?
Or trees that purify the air
To teach us how to thrive and share?

Trustees of wealth, we hold in trust
To make the earth secure and just.
Both rich and poor are blessed for this.
We all can be philanthropists.

I completed my doctorate of divinity, DMin, in 1975 and in 1976. I was called back to Union Theological Seminary as full professor of worship and homiletic, associate professor, of worship and homiletics—the art and science of sermon preparation and delivery.

I taught for thirteen years at Union in the late 1970s and throughout the 1980s. When I first started, I was still pastor in a one-Sunday-a-month church in Roxboro, North Carolina. My father [James A. Forbes Sr.] had been the pastor of that church; then in 1960 he moved to New York City to pastor the famed New Covenant Temple in Harlem on Amsterdam Avenue. He asked me, would I be willing to take that church. So for nine years, while I was a professor at Union, I would travel once a month back to North Carolina to the church at Roxboro.

In the spring of 1976, Don and Peggy Shriver welcomed the Forbes family to the Union Theological Seminary community. Professor Linda Clark and I were invited to share leadership in teaching, preaching, and worship. That appointment led to over forty years of ministry on Morningside Heights of New York City. Three buildings would be the primary locations of my vocation for all the years since, in what turned out to be a remarkable center of learning and service: The Union Seminary Quadrangle, The Riverside Church, and the Interchurch Center on Riverside Drive.

This essay was my opportunity to express gratitude to the Shrivers for their friendship and support across the years. Out of my teaching and preaching experience on Broadway, Claremont Avenue, and Riverside Drive, I have come to a most important theological insight that I am delighted to include in this festschrift in President Shriver's honor. The insight emerged from events connected with the renovation of James Memorial Chapel at Union, the question of updating the communications system in the nave of The Riverside Church, and the question of the architectural design of the Interchurch Center—later referred to as "The God Box." In each of these situations a uniting problematic was the issue of what I choose to call "Divine Aesthetics."

When I arrived at Union Seminary in 1958, it was my daily practice to worship in James Chapel. Its Scottish Gothic divided chancel and neatly ordered cushioned pews made it feel like the "holy of holies." One felt the very presence of God just by entering that hallowed space. I had no difficulty therefore understanding the fierce resistance from many when the decision was made in 1979 to renovate the chapel space to remove the divided chancel, the stately organ with impressive ranks of pipes, the ornate pulpit with its eagle wings lectern, and the beautiful, paneled walls. The entire space was to be commissioned, approved to be configured according to the various traditions now calling the chapel a place of worship. The liturgical space would be staged to accommodate the symbolism and style of worship on an ad hoc basis. Staff and equipment would be made available to work with members of the alternating worship planning committees. No particular tradition could claim exclusive domain; all would be free to prepare the meeting space for the encounter with the divine presence. What a powerful theological question such newly acquired freedom placed before all of us. What kind of space best satisfies the divine taste?

In 1989, I accepted the call to be the senior minister of the famed Riverside Church right across the street from the seminary. Words are inadequate to describe the beauty and majesty of the procession of nearly three hundred robed clergy representing a vast interfaith array of ministerial colleagues who had been assembled on June 1 of that year to launch Riverside into its interracial reconciliation and prophetic rededication to peace, justice, and compassion. I suspect there was even angelic representation that evening as we entered one of the most wonderful worship spaces since Chartres Cathedral was dedicated in France in the thirteenth century. The music was ethereal and the Rev. Gardner Taylor bellowed forth words of hope for new and exciting happenings on Morningside Heights. In the course of time, we were rudely awakened to how difficult it is to bring heaven down to earth and to sustain even sin—for long. In a few months some members discovered, "Oh my God... He's Black!" There was a difference in style between Coffin and Forbes. People started responding to the sermons with "Amen!" and "Hallelujah!" Was the music going to change? And why does it take so long for the Spirit to get around to the point? How long will it be before we hit the tilt factor. Turning Riverside into just another Black church in Harlem?

One of the complications in the transition had to do with the sound system and the newly accelerated pace of proclamation. The beauty of the space in terms of sight left something to be desired concerning sound. It was suggested that the quality of the sound might be improved if we mounted speakers on the columns of the nave—color coordinated, of course, to blend in with the gray interior of the church. But then it was brought to our attention that there was a formal prohibition from affixing anything to the walls of the church, or even inscribing new information there. What good is it to fiercely maintain the visual beauty of a worship space if doing so inhibits the transmission of God's word? I thought, here that question is again: "What kind of space best satisfies the divine taste?"

Then I remembered that in 1958 we had gathered at the corner of Riverside Drive and what was then West 120th Street (later named Reinhold Niebuhr Place) to dedicate the Interchurch Center. It was an imposing structure appropriate in size to the Gothic tower of The Riverside Church right across the street. President Dwight D. Eisenhower had presided over the laying of the cornerstone. As I stood with the crowd observing the ceremony from the shade of Riverside Park, I was struck by the utter absence of ornamentation or stylistic distinction of the building. It was like a big box. What led to the choice of that design for a building that was to house the major denominations of the church and also serve the sacred agencies of the community? It will be no surprise to anyone that some form of our personal question had been considered in the final choice of the architectural design. From Paula M. Mayo, President and Executive Director of the present-day Interchurch Center, I learned that it was Mr. John D. Rockefeller's desire to provide a building that could be for all denominations. No one denomination was to view the building as representing its traditions. There was to be equality in the sense of shared claim to the space. It was to be a place where there was family reunion to do the Lord's work. Among the various proposals submitted, the one that won out had the distinction that no one could call it uniquely her or his own. It would be theirs together. If it looks like a box, so be it. Might even that kind of bland space satisfy the divine taste?

IN 1984, WHILE still teaching at Union Theological Seminary, I was invited by the Church of the Covenant to be a speaker at their Mid-Winter Ministers Conference; it was held in Minneapolis, Minnesota. I was headed to Atlanta on Delta airlines to speak for the Lutheran Church. Their rostered ministers have about a thousand preachers of the Lutheran Church. The ministers were really asking me to speak to them on how they could finally begin to end racism in their church.

I was glad to have that assignment.

In preparation, I looked at my books of reference, and there were two books that I had pulled off the shelf. One was by James D. G. Dunn. His book focused on the book of Romans. In that book, he presented how the first part of Romans was based on life as it was lived through the people of Israel in the second half. Specifically, God was saying to Paul, "I beseech you brethren that you present your bodies as a living sacrifice holy acceptable."

Which is to say not just some ministry to Israel but to Gentiles.

I had also pulled from the shelf the book "History and Spirit" by Joel Kovel, in which he had written that the problem of our society was that we had become a despiritualized society. So, his notion of spiritualization became very important. I had read it over, and I was going to review it again on this trip. Maybe while on the plane, I would try to read. (Joel Kovel is not exactly easy to read.) I tried to see if I could really understand what he meant, this spiritualization?

I had come to the point where it was beginning to emerge with clarity that by de-spiritualized, he meant the reconnection of spirit to its vital connection. A reconnection to sources of value, meaning to have accountability and responsibility to environmental hospitality and fundamental aspects of emotional, psychic, natural, and Divine relationality. I assessed Joel Kovel to be saying that when you lose vital connection to that it's a matter of despiritualization and that our society as a postmodern society has reached that point. Spirit values and the unifying forces of community were lacking and we were more materialistically focused on the exclusion of spiritual values, so that dispelled the notion that it was going to be traditional evangelism. In fact, my work would not be primarily evangelistic at all in the traditional sense of my attempt to renew the spirit of the nation. Actually, it would be designed to help the culture open up its heart to the reality of God and Spirit as it affects the unfolding of the democratic principles by which our society would flourish. I had been reading Kovel when I fell asleep, and when I opened my eyes, I came back to myself, seeing forms and figures such as the symbols of formulas or science: mathematical symbols, some letters, numbers, signs, etc. By the time I was fully awake, my spirit says,

"The kind of spiritual renewal that I have in mind for you has to do not simply with religion, but the multiple elements that make up a society."

My accommodations were in a hotel in Saint Paul. The morning that I was supposed to go to do the speech was a very cold day. I mean very cold! The driver called me and explained, "I will be picking you up shortly; we're delayed just a bit." Well, because it was so cold, I told him, "Well, thank you very much. I'm going to stay in my room until you arrive because it's so cold. Just call me when you arrive."

While I was waiting in my room, I knelt down to pray. I mean, I was glad to have this uncharacteristically free moment. I said to myself, "let me get down on my knees and use this time to say some prayers."

So, I got on my knees and I began to talk to God about how busy I was, how frantic my schedule was—I mean, I'm running all over the place; and I said,

> *"I need to get greater clarity about what God wants me to do with my life." I said to God, "at the pace I'm going, I could be dead by the time I'm fifty years old."*

Having not yet discovered the focus of my work or the trajectory of my journey . . .

> *"I mean, so far what is the central mission You have for me, and I am just raising the question?"*

Sometimes when I'm speaking, I'll conduct a gentle hand clap to express what I am feeling. So as I clapped my hands—you know, with the frustration of being overly busy—I said in coordination with my clap . . .

> *"What (clap) do You (clap) want me (clap) to do (clap) with my life (clap)?"*

In my spirit, the response to me was . . .

> *"I have heard your petition, and I am responding to your question in the form (physical and sound)*

> *of the cadence of your hand clapping. Your hand clapping is about the cadence of the clap."*

So, I clap them again, as I had been doing, and I said . . .

> *". . . yes, I hear the cadence. What is the meaning of the cadence?"*

The answer in my spirit was this . . .

> *". . . the spiritual renewal of the nation is that to which I have called you."*

I thought that God was saying to me, perhaps, you're going to be a great evangelist, like Billy Graham, or maybe a cross between Billy Graham and Martin Luther King Jr. So, I was looking forward to focusing in that direction. I believed that my effectiveness was going to be based on my functioning according to that assignment, "The spiritual renewal of the nation is that to which I have called you."

It was not until 2017, more than twenty years later, after my call to Riverside Church and nearly a decade after I retired from Riverside, that I got full clarity about what "the spiritual renewal of the nation" meant. My life has been and is dedicated to the respiritualization of the nation. I have, since I retired from

Riverside Church, embarked on that part of my journey by founding Healing of the Nations Foundation (HON), a national nonprofit, faith-based corporation that creates transformative dialogues and events to heal the wounds of racial, religious, and economic injustice festering in our nation. I am glad to know that God still speaks to my spirit, and my soul is prepared to honor what I am told. I see signs of God's agape love, better days ahead.

Excellence! Excellence! Excellence!

> Oh Lord, how excellent is Your name in
>   all the earth.
> You endowed creation with excellence
>   from its birth.
> All things in Your image have excellence
>   imprinted.
> Every human heart has some excellence
>   within it.
>
> Overshadow us Lord with glorious majesty
> Until Your holy excellence every eye can see.
> Anoint with your spirit each fiber of my
>   heart.
> Release in us the excellence You gave us
>   from the start.

Chorus

Excellence! Excellence! Excellence!
Let's make excellence our aim.
We were made for excellence,
In God's majestic name.

I STAYED AT Union for thirteen years, until in 1989, when I accepted the call to The Riverside Church, the first African American Senior Minister of the church. While at Union Theological Seminary, I received the honor of being requested by President Shapiro of Princeton University to become the chaplain of the University Chapel, and I was offered a wonderful contract. I was on the verge of accepting that prestigious assignment; however, Bill Coffin at Union Theological Seminary decided to retire, and people who were my friends said, "Man, why don't you throw your name in the hat? Maybe you might get a nod, you never know?" So, I had to think hard about this, because you know, Princeton University is offering me this wonderful contract. I think I'd be a fool to turn Princeton University down! My spirit said, "the issue if you are attempting to get started on the spiritual renewal of the nation is to consider in which location might you experience a more fruitful path toward that end?" I thought and decided maybe with the bully pulpit of The Riverside Church, I might be able to make headway in my work of attempting to promote the spiritual renewal of the nation.

So, I called Dr. Shapiro and declined the invitation to be the chaplain at Princeton Chapel, and instead, I chose to go to The Riverside Church. From time to time, people would ask me, *how is the revival going?* They viewed the spiritual renewal of the nation as a revival. Throughout the years, I had to say not yet.

Riverside was created by wealthy white New Yorkers. When John D. Rockefeller asked the Rev. Harry Emerson Fosdick about creating a church, Fosdick requested a church in Harlem to simultaneously serve white and Black people. At the time, I was fifty-three years old and a professor of preaching at Union Theological Seminary when I was chosen from over two-hundred candidates to be the fifth senior minister of Riverside Church and the first Black person to serve as a senior minster.

I served a divided congregation at The Riverside Church. My leadership and preaching style was celebrated and rejected at the same time. In 1993, I was recognized by *Ebony* magazine as one of the nation's top preachers. In 1996, *Newsweek* recognized me as one of the twelve most effective preachers in the English-speaking world. My work was to elevate spiritual awareness in the church and in the public square. Riverside thus became a career milestone and a period of great challenge. I had to walk with God intimately to sustain my faith. During this time, I affirmed God is in Spirit in the church, in our relationships, in our community, and in the issues of the day.

Doctor, Tell Me Why?

Doctor, tell me why my tongue is so sore,
    and my stomach feels so tight.

Your tongue is sore because you bite your
    tongue each time you're insulted,
and your ego is stung!

You're afraid to speak out for fear of
    further abuse.

So, you bridle and bite your tongue,
    saying what's the use.

Meanwhile, your tongue is bleeding and
    starting to flow into a pool of
resentment in your stomach below.

It collects into a pool of unexpressed rage
    and if you're not careful, it may
reach a dangerous stage.

Poisoning your body, your psyche, and
>   your spirit too—that's what biting
your tongue can do to you.

Therefore, I advise you to free your tongue
>   each day, to speak what you feel
though retribution may come your way.

Your tongue will get well, and your stomach
>   will feel great; then your mind,
tongue, and stomach will be free to celebrate.

I'm Living in Hope

I'm living in hope.
The Lord will see us through.
The God we serve will show us what to do.
No matter what my enemies do or say.
I'm living in hope to see a brighter day.

Now faith is the substance of things
>   hoped for
The evidence of things not seen.
Put your trust in the love of our never-
>   failing God.
Steady yourself, press your way, the Lord
>   will intervene.

I'm living in hope.
The Lord will see us through.
The God we serve will show us what to do.
No matter what my enemies do or say,
I'm living in hope to see a brighter day.

You may be uncertain of health, jobs, or
    friends
Desperately reaching for a helping hand.
Burdened down, all stressed out,
Heartbroken and confused.
God steps in, takes your hand, and gives
    you strength to stand.

I'm living in hope.
The Lord will see us through.
The God we serve will show us what to do.
No matter what my enemies do or say,
I'm living in hope to see a brighter day.

Live in hope my sister
Live in hope my brother
Hope in God is the only way
To make it to a brighter day

Live in hope in the city.
Live in hope across the nation.

Calling all the whole creation.
Live, oh live in hope.
Live oh live,
Live in hope.

I'm living in hope.
The Lord will see us through.
The God we serve will show us what to do.
No matter what my enemies do or say,
I'm living in hope to see a brighter day.

Golden Moments of Kindness

Put selfish deeds, meanness, and greed away
Make room for justice and kindness each
    day
Let thoughtfulness replace indifference
Dare to achieve a new significance

Each call to improve bad situations
Allows us to cure one of life's complications
When the door of "NOW" closes, no reprieve
That golden moment we cannot retrieve

The world is desperate for hints of grace
Why prolong the nightmares of class and
    race

When hope and healing cry out for a friend
You could be the one to let the light in

Let's resolve to embrace each random chance
For tender-loving care to be enhanced
Now is the time for world repair
Start kindness revolutions everywhere

In This Special Holy Place

This is a house of blessings
Come and have your souls refreshed
Let the love of the Spirit fill your heart
In this house, you are special guests

Welcome—your newborn babies
Welcome—all the children, too
Greet your friends and your neighbors
    with these words
"There's a blessing here for you."

Bring all your fears and failures
All your doubts and deep distress
Then with childlike assurance, bring your
    dreams
God is here, let us all be blessed

Chorus
We are blessed to be in your presence
In this ark of love and grace
We are blessed to be invited guests
In this special holy place

We are blessed to be in your presence
In this consecrated space
We are blessed to have our souls refreshed
In this special holy place

An Ode to Me, We, and Thee

I used to pray to a God above,
One I could not see, so removed from me.
A mystical power who commands us to love,
But punishes us for our iniquity.

Recently, I had a new discovery,
About a comprehensive deity.
God has revealed a sacred enormity—
The one God: Me, We, and Thee.

This God is ultimate relationality.
Thee emits power to all Creation.
The Holy Spirit empowers you and me,
And spreads through the universe—equality.

All praise to the God of Eternity,
To the God of Me, We, and Thee.
Let us dance a new choreography:
Joyful, loving, and forever free.

Everybody Let's Get Ready

Chorus
Everybody let's get ready for our mansion above
There's a golden crown for everyone who will live in the spirit of love.

Verse 1
We're commanded to love the Lord, our God
And to love our neighbors too
The neighbor you hate, will wait at the gate
To put bad mouth on you
In the Bible, we're warned to tell the truth
Our God can't stand a liar
A lying tongue is the devil's tool
To set the world on fire

Chorus

Verse 2
The good book tells us to bless the poor

With hope for a brighter day
When Saint Peter asks you "What did
    you do?"
You'd better have something to say
No stealing, no dealing, no games of greed
No stirring up hate and fear
At the pearly gates, there's a great big sign
"No haters allowed up here!"

Chorus

Verse 3
A judging spirit leaves a poisonous sting
It keeps resentment alive
A wall to exclude is a dangerous thing
It can block what you need to survive
When people dress up in selfish pride
The Lord can hardly bear it
You hypocrite, you know your crown
    won't fit
Your head's too big to wear it

Chorus

CODA
On that Judgment Day, I hope to hear
    God say

"Come and put on your golden crown—
   The Crown of Love."

Thank You Jesus for Being There for Me

Thank You Jesus for being there for me.
When the shadow of death was closing in
   on me.
Your loving hands reached down to lift
   me up.
I've got to thank You for being there for me.

You set me free, Jesus. You set me free.
No more condemnation, my spirit is free!
You delivered my soul from bondage with
   Your call to liberty:
"Go in peace, sin no more; I'm dying to
   set you free."

Thank You Jesus for being there for me.
Thank You for your tender, loving care for
   me.
Thanks for being a lawyer to plead my case.
Thank You for the verdict: "Saved by grace!"
Doctor Jesus, I thank You for fixing my
   heart.

Thank You for the gift of a brand-new
    start.
Precious Savior, I really love You. You
    gave your life for me.
I want the whole wide world to know:
    You are my Jubilee.

Repeat
I'll praise Your name forever and serve
    You eternally.
Thank You, my blessed Redeemer, for
    being there for me.

Never Give Up on You

You've been struggling and striving so.
Trying to choose which way to go.
You pray to God, "Help me to stand!"
Temptation reaches for your hand.

You feel foolish, each vow you make.
Oh, what strength recovery takes.
The sweet relief from all that pain
Makes you fall again and again.

There's no question, you have to change.
Some special help must be arranged.

Please don't say "once more, then I'm
 through."
This time death could be stalking you.

You may cry, "there's no hope for me."
Let me die in my misery.
But another voice makes this plea:
There's more for you, listen to me.

Chorus
Never give up and never lose heart.
The strength is within you to make a new
 start.
Although you have fallen lower than low,
With no one to care and no place to go,
The Spirit whispers, "You'll make it through.
I love you, and I'll never let go of you."

"I really, really love you and I'll never ever
Let go of you."

In 1997, while on sabbatical from The Riverside Church, I was given a grant by the Henry Luce Foundation to teach a course on urban ministry at Harvard Divinity School. During that time of refreshing, I had the most wonderful experience.

Everything seemed to work toward my aspirations. I was so frequently blessed; everything that I needed was provided. I wrote a poem to express my profound gratitude for the many blessings I was receiving. I inquired of God what I could do to show how deeply grateful I was. This poem provides the answer God gave me.

LOVE MY CHILDREN

I looked around the other day and saw
How truly blessed this life of mine has
    been.
I have health, strength, and comfort,
Peace and joy within.

Care in times of desperation.
A helping hand when friends are few.
And so, I asked, "Dear Lord, what can I do
To return some thanks to you?"

I expected mission impossible
A call to service far away.
But instead, this gentle assignment,
God sends to us each day:

"Love my children—
that's all I ask of you.

Love my children—that's what you've got
    to do.
If you love them as I love them,
We shall see them safely through."

"Respect them, protect them
Uphold them, enfold them
Affirm the gifts inside of them
Until they learn to take pride in them."

"If they falter, if they stray,
Don't lose heart, find another way.
Never, ever count them out.
That's what love is all about."

"Love yourself, love Me too. Love the ones
    who are close to you.
Love the One who has brought you through.
And whatever else you do . . .

Love my children."

Thank You for Making and Mending Me for Love—a Prayer

Sovereign God, loving Spirit, I offer praise to you, for making me who I've been called to be and to do what I should do: gentle, compassionate, kind, and fair, and for making me who I've been. And this is the land that I've helped to change, so that's why I'm here today. Thank you for making me who I've been and for doing what I should do: gentle, compassionate, kind, and fair; eager to get along and ready to share; alert to the needs of others, especially the poor and oppressed. If I can help somebody, I try to do my very best. When I've been offended, I stand ready to reconcile. I'm inclined to greet my enemies with a forgiving smile.

But when guns, weapons of war, and the spirit of hostility threatened the peace of the planet, some tried to deny or ignore it. Still others were plunged into despair and panic. You saw civilization poised on the brink of devastation and decided to come out of hiding to address the situation. You chose me to help you spread love everywhere, but before I could begin, you had to mend my heart from a serious tear. Principalities and powers still fight against the beloved community. The ministry of love requires boldness, courage, and integrity.

I had become an expert in avoiding conflict and contention, a master of feigning acceptance of what called for dissension. My inner thoughts were one thing, public expressions bordered on fraud. Was my caution designed to protect me from other folks' convictions? Or was my timidity from fear of suffering the prophets' afflictions? When one proclaims God's truth, one may be subject to vilification. That's the price you have to pay when you accept the prophetic vocation.

Dear God, you reminded me of your preference for profanity rather than a niceness that covered up rage on the verge of insanity. The psalmist said you desire truth in the inward parts. You can't stand lies that emanate from our hearts. It is better to be angry and tell the truth about what you feel, than to try and seem righteous and keep the truth concealed. Near my ninetieth birthday, while you made plans to save society, you took the best of my old self and started making a more courageous me.

God has been tugging with all creation to live in the spirit of love, pulling us together to be one family: the earth below and the stars above. I felt that calling and considered myself to be in Love's family. The Spirit took me, refined me, and is teaching me the joy of harmony. Have you felt the tug to join God's dream team of love evolution? Has the coach, the Spirit, revealed shortcomings in your personal constitution? Are you being empowered for the game of cosmic touch and tag, where we are becoming who we were destined to be, without a lag?

To all my friends who knew me in my former iteration, rejoice with me that I've had a radical transformation. I'm proud of who I used to be but exhilarated by my emerging liberty. Hallelujah, what a joy to be born again—again, fully free. This new me may fuss, cuss, or discuss vehemently. I may shout, speak in tongues, or prophesy fervently. Let's celebrate God's unending mending until the setting of the sun and listen together to hear God say, "WELL DONE!"

IN AUGUST OF 2023 one of my parishioners from Riverside Church died and requested that I do the eulogy at his funeral, which was to be held on Martha's Vineyard.

In the airport I stopped by the bookstore to pick up a book to read on the journey. A small pocket-sized book caught my eye. It was entitled *Seven Brief Lessons on Physics*, by Carlo Rovelli. I read the book of eighty-one pages on the way to the Vineyard. By the time I finished it, I felt I had been born again, again—that I had had a double anointing of the Spirit.

It was exhilaratingly transformative of my consciousness to the extent that I felt that I was a new person after reading the text. As the book cover indicates, it was a "mind-bending introduction to modern physics." The author described Einstein's general theory of relativity and boggling aspects of quantum mechanics. He explained the architecture of the universe, elementary particle science, quantum gravity, probability, and the heat of black holes and the nature of human consciousness. All these areas he addressed in interesting and easily understandable language that the average person could grasp. As a scientist myself, it was most exciting to be brought up to date on the latest discoveries in the field of physics.

But it was not so much the scientific insights that altered my consciousness. It was what the Spirit was pointing out to me about the nature of God, the beginning of creation, the radical freedom of human beings, the impending calamity of civilization itself, the future of humanity, and our responsibilities to each other and the other orders of creation. Eventually God began to speak to me about what the divine love was going to do to save society and a role that was expected of me in the rescue of civilization from its headlong plunge into degradation.

Walter Edison Lowe in his death had willed to me the unfulfilled aspects of his existence. It gave me the sense that we might expect that when friends and loved ones depart this life, we may become recipients of some special grace they have bequeathed to those who remain.

Walter and I called each other "stent brothers," because both of us had received stents for our nearly collapsed arteries on several occasions. I have three stents in my descending artery, which had been discovered by my cardiologist to be 80 percent clogged. I told Walter that my three stents represented the Father, Son, and Holy Ghost. Perhaps that is why he could entrust to me the unfinished work of being a servant of the Most High God. Nevertheless, God has called me to an agape love of God, which is in each of us whether we know it or not. The death of this friend arranged new life for me.

Whether or Not

I'm going to take heart and get moving
Though the clouds hang heavy and gray.
If I wait for blue-skied perfection
I'll be waiting 'til Judgment Day.

Why let myself be held hostage
Trapped and blocked by who-knows-what?
Will standing in sinking sand
Reverse my fate? Certainly not!

I'm going to break out and risk living
Though the reasons to wait still abound.
I will do what I can in the climate of now,
Till better days roll around.

Chorus
So, take heart my sisters and brothers
Give worries a holiday.
Away with your reasons, delaying the season
Celebration is the order of the day.

Cel-le-ella-bella-bration
Is the or-or-or order of the day!

Zion, Beautiful Zion

Chorus
Zion, Beautiful Zion
I am on my way
I can hardly wait to enter Your Gate
On that blessed day
We shall beat our swords into plowshares
Down by the blissful shore
When we get home
We'll shout SHALOM
And study war no more

Verse 1
By Babylon streams, we refused to sing,
    our joyful Zion songs
Our hymns of praise, we could not raise,
    amid abuse and wrongs
Our prophets cried out, "Hold on to your
    faith, deliverance will come
Lift up your eyes, beyond the skies, that's
    where our help comes from"

Chorus

Verse 2

When our days are rough, and times so
    tough, we cannot see our way
When our hopes and dreams, are replaced
    by screams, of anguish and dismay
When our songs are silenced by hateful
    rage that takes our breath away
Remember the Word, our spirit has
    heard, there'll be a brighter day

Chorus

A Melody of Praise

This song I'm singing is for my special friend.
To the one who gave me life, this hymn l
    raise.
From the bottom of my heart, I am lifting
    up my voice
To sing to God a melody of praise.

Dear Lord, my God, you've been so good
    to me.
You made me in your image, then you set
    my spirit free.
You have always seen more good in me
    than I have been aware.

When down and out and filled with
> doubt, you're the answer to my prayer.

Alpha and Omega, you're the one who
> makes me whole.
My all-sufficient Comforter, you're the
> keeper of my soul.
Mighty Rock of ages, you always see me
> through.
That's why I dedicate this song to the one
> and only God.

I praise you in the morning, I praise you
> all day long.
And even when I go to sleep, my heart
> keeps singing this song.
I praise you when everything's all right,
> when in trouble this is my vow.
No matter how bleak my circumstance,
I'm going to praise you anyhow.
In the way that I walk, in the way that I talk;
In the way that I think, and in the way
> that I pray.
In everything I do, I want to honor you
By the way I live each day.

RACISM IS A plague that threatens the life of our nation. There is a plague in America. It's not the bubonic plague that wiped out 60 percent of the population of Europe over the course of two hundred years, spread by infected rats then bitten by fleas who in turn bit humans. That plague was known as the Black Death.

No, America has its own plague, a plague of racism that could be known as Black Death but in fact it threatens *all* of our health: Black, white, brown, and beyond. This plague has lasted more than four hundred years, beginning with the diseased rats of slavery, lynch mobs, and Jim Crow segregation, spread by the disease flea bites or snake bites of white supremist ideology, oppression, an equal education, and lack of opportunity. Dr. Martin Luther King Jr. observed that we must learn to live together as brothers and sisters, or we will perish as fools. The plague of racism in our nation will lead to our collective downfall unless we diagnose it, treat it, and learn to prevent it.

Like many diseases, the plague of racism has lain dormant in some areas, at times, yet has continued to infect our nation prior to the most recent flareup of symptoms: tragic deaths, detainment, maltreatment and miscarriage of justice for Black men, women, boys, and girls at the hands of the dominant power structure. We would be in some denial if we imagined that our nation had been cured of racism prior to these most recent incidents. They are merely like CAT scans but shot on smartphones and dash cams revealing the disease, the dis-ease, that lies within our body politic and our population.

Life-threatening illness typically leads one through a spectrum of emotional responses, from denial to anger, bargaining, depression, and finally acceptance of the truth. Each of us may find ourselves in a different place in that process of coming to terms with the life-threatening plague of racism in our nation. But the good news is that this plague is not necessarily terminal if we diagnose it, treat it, and speak to prevent its spread. To that end, as the founder of the Healing of Nations Foundation and the National Minister of the Drum Major Institute, I invite our nation into a time of preaching, teaching, conversation, and Bible study in the hope of healing so that we can finally put an end to the plague infecting our nation.

The Prophetic Justice Principles

We, the members of faith communities in the United States, inspired by the Hebrew prophets, lift up the following questions to test public policy against the principles of righteousness and justice in our society.

We ask the citizens and leaders of America to bear the following issues in mind as they seek to restore the spiritual, moral, and democratic values upon which our nation was built.

1. Seek the common good: Does the policy represent the common good of society rather than the interest of an elite few?
2. Be truthful in facts and motives: Is the policy based on true analysis and does it disclose its true intention? How likely is the outcome to achieve its proposed purpose?
3. Promote unity and inclusion: Does the policy hold the prospect of reducing the polarization and fragmentation of the society due to race, religion, class, gender, sexual orientation, or national origin?
4. Care for the poor: Does the policy provide good news for the poor? Does it reverse the trend toward an ever-widening gap between rich and poor?

5. Protect the vulnerable: Is the policy good for children, the elderly, and the disadvantaged? Does it show sensitivity to the spirit of the golden rule?
6. Guard freedom of thought and discussion: Does the policy provide for free press, free discussion, and the expression of dissent along with fair and just methods of participation in the democratic process?
7. Respect other nations and peoples: Does the policy encourage respect for peoples and nations other than our own? Does it respect the fundamental dignity and rights of every human being? Does it use diplomacy as a valued instrument of statecraft in resolving international conflicts and refrain from unilateral military actions for empire-building and domination strategies?
8. Ensure stewardship of creation: Is the policy supportive of strong measures to ensure ecological responsibility and sustainability?
9. Cherish the human family: Does the policy practice good global citizenship involving respect for all cultures and nations, and collective responsibility for the common good of the global community? Does it refrain from nationalism, militarism, or imperialism based on a sense of national superiority?

10. Provide moral leadership: Does the policy lead by example, doing the right thing and holding the right lessons for our children and our citizens? Does it promote a more ethical society and uphold trust in public offices?

Racism is such a shameful thing that practitioners often tend to avoid any exchange or any public discussion of it. They'd rather keep their sinister perspectives to themselves. This poem is my effort to bring them out of denial about it and to create an occasion for sincere reflection with an honest conversation about race.

A Conversation with Our Nation About Race

Is it true that an idea that's not true
has captured our minds, causing some to
    see themselves as superior
and others of lower stock?

No doubt! It creeps in almost everywhere:
mean jokes and jeers in clan privacy,
black codes and secret zones in the public
    square.

Bruises branding some as cursed by birth,
and privileged abundance claims proof of
    God's choice
for those to be vice-regents on earth.

Is the mere thought of race, a viral
    infection stealthily invading?
Or are your private conversations much
    like microbial particles
subliminally masquerading as quantum
    intelligence, infiltrating as light waves?

From this affliction, these symptoms appear:
denial and regret,
guilt and remorse,
resentment and oppression,
fear and aggression.

Naming the disease makes people feel
    shame.
Muted, it's racism all the same.
This xenophobic ideology brings mischief,
    murder, and brutality.

While living within the lie, character is
    flawed.
Masks are contrived to cover up the fraud.

Self-defense is strong—truth even stronger.
Once aware, hard to bear any longer.

Who Do We Think We Are?

Who do we think we are as a nation?
Too exceptional to falter or lose?
Even when we blow it—and we all
    know it
We will find somebody else to accuse.

Those who view masks and vaccines as
    gimmicks,
And dare to tell the virus to bug off,
Are ruthlessly putting us all at risk
Refusing to cover our sneeze or our cough.

Fellow citizens, let us humbly pledge
Not to bring our planet to a fatal end.
By cruel selfishness and thoughtless deeds
Acting in ways no sane person can defend.

Lord, please deliver us from this awful
    mess:
Blasphemous deeds from hearts of stone.
Until by your grace, our nation is blessed,
The American dream will ache and groan.

Rap Response

Alcohol, heroin, coke, and fentanyl
Propofol and Demerol—all those pills,
I might as well come clean and then confess
I'm hooked, I'm cooked, I'm a pitiful mess.

It's quite the same with other afflictions.
Bigotry is an evil addiction:
Hating, race-baiting, supremacy drunk
Reveals that your heart and mind have
    shrunk.

Condemning others in their malaise
Keeps you from facing your own sick ways.
We all need rehabilitation
From our own despiritualization.

Let's go get treated for recovery
And claim our full humanity.
Forgiveness and tender-loving care
Is what it's gonna take to get us there.

No Time for Foolishness

Airplanes falling, peace talks stalling
Smallpox, Anthrax, looking like the flu
Throat grabbing, backstabbing

Kids getting high on drugs and glue
Short graves, long graves, you never know
    which
Electrocuting men just to see them twitch

Now I don't mean to be uncouth
All I'm asking for is tell me the truth!
What time is it, y'all?
No time for foolishness.

Cops profiling—Supreme Court smiling
Politicians playing games just to be in
    control
Wealthy getting richer, poor getting poorer
With rats and homeless living in the sewer
Housing prices going sky high
Nothing to rent and can't afford to buy.

Now I don't mean to be uncouth
All I'm asking for is tell me the truth!
What time is it, y'all?
No time for foolishness

Affirmative action under attack
You bring your money home, but there's a
    hole in the sack
Spousal, parental, systems abuse

Sometimes you wonder, what's the use?
COVID is spreading like an eating cancer
Nations call for help, but there's no answer.

Now I don't mean to be uncouth
All I'm asking for is tell me the truth!
What time is it, y'all?
No time for foolishness

Races and religions all self-contained
High blood pressure from too much strain
Why are our families falling apart?
We went searching for pleasure and lost
  our heart
Hope and love are in short supply
We've got to find our purpose or else
  we'll die

Now I don't mean to be uncouth
All I'm asking for is tell me the truth!
What time is it, y'all?
No time for foolishness

When True Healing Has Begun

Oh, how precious is the freedom which
  through struggle has been won.

Sweeter yet the celebration when true
    healing has begun.
First the healing of the spirit, of a people
    torn apart.
Tattered ties of friendship mended, trust
    restored in every heart.

Reconnect us, Ancient Spirit. Bring
    forgiveness, love, and power.
Teach us how to be one people. Guide us
    through this birthing hour.
Bid us reach across the chasm—class and
    culture, tribe and race.
Help us see in hearts of others, hopes and
    dreams we all embrace.

From the evils of oppression, Lord,
    deliver and redeem.
When we fear for retribution, cleanse us
    with Your love supreme.
Courage calls for true confession—how
    our sins have maimed us so.
Hope inspires a new direction, reaching
    out to friend and foe.

While we dream and build together, heart
    to heart and hand in hand.

Well, uncover hidden treasures, lavished on our blessed land.
None alone can reap the harvest, all our stories hold a key
To the age of hope and healing; peaceful, just, secure, and free.

On how precious is the freedom which through struggle has been won.
Sweeter yet the celebration when true healing has begun.
By God's grace we lift our voices. Many tongues will sing one song.
Once divided, now united, Lo! A nation free and strong!

Love's Response to the Crisis of the Nation

I am usually hiding in the deep recesses of anonymity
In the invisible corner of my infinity,
But sometimes the frightening prediction of the end of civilization
Prompts me to arrange a love-directed revelation.

I see, hear, and feel groanings in the
    global community.
"Have mercy, oh God, deliver us from all
    forms of incivility.
Save us from the pandemic of greed, lust
    for power, and tyranny.
Don't let us lose sight of justice and
    genuine humanity."

Vanishing values and character flaws
    bespeak spiritual death.
Kindness and compassion seem to be
    running out of breath.
Though civilization may stand on a most
    slippery slope
Hear my voice of assurance and find fresh
    cause for hope.

Now I must break out of hiddenness to
    make myself known,
I must transform human consciousness
    before all hope is gone.
I will remind the world of what in
    creation I was dreaming of:
A mutually affirming humanity held
    together by my love.

This is my wake-up call to all, "Rise from
    mistrust and fear."
Embrace your destiny to make my image clear.
The spirit, you, and I a mystical unity
Building together the blessed, beloved
    community.

For those who are not sure what the
    beloved community is, let me explain.
It is the dream for a just society that God
    had in mind at the dawn of creation.

So, you see God had a dream too, as
    Archbishop Desmond Tutu's book
    declared.

When God is Acknowledged as God Again

When God is acknowledged as God again
We can confess our original sin.
When truth and justice recover their place
The nation can face the issue of race.

When we cast away selfishness, greed, and
    scorn
The spirit of democracy can be reborn.

When we learn to cherish the comfort of love
Our character will be nourished from above.

God will inspire beloved community,
Making more complete our humanity.
Healing infirmities, we've known from
 birth
Bringing the joy of heaven to earth.

God's Dream of the World

This is the world I've been dreaming of
This is the world I've been looking for
A world I call "beloved community"
Everybody valued, secure and free.

Dedicated to the common good
Diversity welcomed in the neighborhood
No oppression or domination
Justice, the goal of every nation
Love, the only true supremacy
Many ethnicities, one family.

Bigotry condemned as evil and vile
Warfare and sedition out of style
Children respecting and enjoying each other
The needy cared for as sister and brother

The whole atmosphere as sacred space
Creator and created in a loving embrace.

Now that's the kind of world I've been
    dreaming of
That's the kind of world I've been looking for
Wake up and dream along with me
And build the kind of world I intend it to be.

A Sighting of the Hand of God
(A Prophecy)

The Hand of God will soon be seen.
Some will wonder, what does this mean?
Some will rejoice, others lament.
Some will feel the need to repent.

Some may change their way of thinking.
Some may ignore it through drinking.
Some may conspire to deny it.
Some may wish they could defy it.

What e'er may be our reaction,
When God speaks, there is no retraction.
Will we see punishment for bigotry?
God, please renew democracy!

IN OUR MOST intense arguments about gender, many of us appeal to what God wills. However, if the truth be known, what we believe is also impacted by sociological factors as well. Even in the most deeply religious society, rules and regulations about human behavior bear marks of what the community feels is in its best interest. We may think that our arguments are strengthened when we claim that a practice is totally the mandate of God. We are closer to the truth when we acknowledge that the elders of the community, under the guidance of the Spirit, set forth the principles by which the community could survive and thrive. Usually, religious traditions sanctify what society considers necessary, even though perceived necessity changes from time to time. Things that were once condoned but prove to be harmful to the community are usually replaced. Child sacrifice, immolation, and stoning are just a few of the ways sin used to be punished, but no more. The Spirit can lead societies away from harm and toward closer understandings of God's loving will.

We need more free language, truer to the many dimensions and experiences of God disclosed by Jesus, who, in his parables and stories, depicted God as both feminine and masculine. If we cannot call God as "mother," neither can we call God "Father," for female is as much a window on divinity as male.

I'll Be with You 'til the End of Time

I'll be with you 'til the end of time
I'll be with you 'til the end of time
Don't you worry about what your future
    holds
I'll be with you through eternity

I was there when you were nothing
But a thought, a wish and a prayer
In your mother's womb, I saw you
When she didn't even know you were there

The day you were born I was present
You were crying and trembling with fear
Then I smiled and your eyes were opened
Amazed at your new world out here

Through your childhood years, I followed close
While you searched for your purpose and place
In your struggle to reach your lifelong dream
I offered guidance, forgiveness, and grace

So, tell me why would I forsake you now
When I've stood by you through thick and thin
I have chosen you as a dwelling place
For My Spirit to abide within

When your song of life has ended
And the curtains can rise no more
Close your eyes without fear, I'm with you
My arms will lift you to a brighter shore.

I'll be with you 'til the end of time
I'll be with you 'til the end of time
Don't worry about what your future holds
I'll be with you through eternity.

I HAVE A call to action called "Spirit in Our Vote." Our Spirit must be sent forward in our vote. We must make a resounding noise to eradicate hate by speaking to the power of love through our vote. We must elect representation that will stand with the beloved community.

The More Perfect Voter

I get out of bed and take a bath,
Put on my clothes and plan my daily
    path.
Before starting out, I take time to pray.
I speak to God above, and this is what I say:

My Creator, Sustainer, Protector through
    the night.
My Healer, Deliverer, my Guiding Light.
In You I trust, I cast my vote for You.
You're the only one who can see us through.

I'll treat the earth as sacred space,
And call hateful violence—a cruel disgrace.
I'll respect and honor my sisters and brothers.
Not just my kin, but all the others.

I'll work for a world of equality.
Safe and secure for all humanity.
I'll resist domination by the powerful few,
And lift the lowly who put their trust in You.

Then I'll vote for myself as chief executive,
Of the way to think and the way to live.
I'll try to do your will in search for satisfaction,
And take responsibility for my daily actions.

At times, I have pledged You my loyalty,
Then followed a different deity.
But today, I'm casting my vote for You.
Not just with the ballot, but by what I do.

I vote for You because I know You will win.
Love is the solution for the crisis we're in.
Things may not turn out as they ought to be,
But a vote for You is assured victory.

Vote NO! to Hate

Vote NO! to hate and bigotry
The Lord is calling you and me
To be honest to God, happy and free
Let's make our state first in liberty

We are all God's children
Both Black and white
We all are precious in God's sight
Together let's build up community
Make our state first in liberty

Let us cast our vote for a land that's free
To the glory of God and all humanity

Voter Suppression: A Punishable Offense

God gives each of us the power to choose
To vote opinions and express our views.
To show up and vote is our destiny;
It's a sign of our God-given humanity.

Don't tamper with my vote or mute my
    voice.
It's a vile transgression to kill my choice.

When you suppress my vote, you curse
    your soul.
For that, you'll be sentenced without parole.

Will the Supreme Court Honor Our Constitution?

America, what were the just intents
Of the fathers' founding documents?
Whose liberties intended in the red,
    white, and blue?
Red, white, black, and brown or just a few?

More important than the message they sent
Are the values, convictions, and moral content.
If the documents are flawed, don't close
    your eyes.
Congenital defects must be excised.

Let's hold a justice plebiscite
To mend the flaws, to make things right.
Let's honor our dead who set us free
By risking the courage of integrity.

Must we continue the sins of the past?
Dare we acknowledge the truth at last?
An honest nation will humbly change
When conscience sees its past as strange.

A divided house surely cannot stand.
As Lincoln said, "don't divide this land."
The Creator made us for equal grace.
Can our constitution honor every race?

Census Sensibility

When you do a census of the human race
Be sure to reserve everybody a place
God intends that every need be supplied
Nobody naked, hungry, or left outside
It would be a mean and sinister hoax
To treat neighbors as non-existent folks

God is watching the steps we take
Counting others out makes a census fake
Selfishness and greed are fatal afflictions
Just as deadly as opioid addictions
Our nation can't be a democracy
Until she learns to count both you and
    me.

The Winning Vote

Come on everybody, get on the victory
    van
It's waiting here to take you to the
    Promised Land.

No time for procrastination
You can't afford to wait
The polls will soon be closing
You can't risk being late.

The Good Lord has a blessing for you
That will bring you pride and honor too
Other votes have already been cast
History waits for yours at last.

You'll be a hero and wear the victor's coat
Headlines will shout, "You cast the
 winning vote!"

Get on the Path

Get on the path, get on the path, get on
 the path. I'll meet you there.
Let's get on the path and stay on the path.
 The Lord will meet us there.
Get on the path of justice. Get on the
 path of love.
Get on the path of freedom and peace.
 The Lord will meet us there.

To soothe our feet from the rocky road
To lift the weight of our heavy load

To wipe the tears from our weary eyes
To gather all nations for a peace sunrise.

Job got on the path, and the path got hard.
His wife cried out, "Why don't you curse
    your God?"
His so-called friends scandalized his name.
He waited patiently until deliverance came.

Esther the Queen, oh what beauty and grace.
Heard of the plot to destroy her race.
She fasted and prayed, "What path shall I take?
I'll take the path of courage for my
    people's sake."

Martin Luther King, prophet, preacher,
    and priest,
Laid down his life for the last and the least.
With a heart full of love and the touch of
    God's hand,
He pressed his way to the Promised Land.

Can you see the path set before us today?
Do you hear the call to the peace and
    justice way?
Open your heart to the Spirit above.
Join the great procession to the city of love.

MAY WE REMEMBER the quadricentennial of the arrival of Africans on American shores, remembering the words of Genesis 15:13 (NRSV):

> *Then the Lord said to Abram, "Know this for certain, that your offspring shall be aliens in a land that is not theirs and shall be slaves there, and they shall be oppressed for four hundred years; but I will bring judgment on the nation that they serve, and afterward, they shall come out with great possessions."*

Let us explore the deeper theological source and significance of the song, "Lord, How Come Me Here?" Is that a question that would normally be raised by all human beings? Is the question more likely to be raised by those who experience the brutality of dehumanization? Is it possible diminishment of human sensitivity not to raise this question? And in regard to the thought, "I wish I never was born," was it only a fleeting moment of Job-like despair that flashed before all of us when the threat of non-being almost overwhelmed us?

All Americans Together
(A Juneteenth Meditation)

Newly freed slaves were ecstatic on that
    great day.
They thanked God for liberty despite the delay.
God said, "Though you are free from the
    chains of slavery,
You're still captives of a murderous bigotry."

Slave owners were grieving for their lost
    property,
People they had whipped and lynched
    from many a tree.
Though African slaves from bondage were
    now set free,
Slaveholders were still slaves to white
    supremacy.

God spoke to those called "white" down
    from heaven on high,

"Your tribe has been disgraced by a
    demonizing lie.
As slavery ends, so must each barbaric crime.
Repent! Repair! Accept forgiveness while
    there's time."

From whence that vile delusion came, it
    has to go.
Never forget you shall surely reap what
    you sow.
The higher power of justice will not relent.
It will fulfill the purpose for which it was
    sent.

While the Spirit makes truth and love its
    demand,
Depraved and sick souls suppress justice
    in the land.
We must decide the convictions we will
    embrace
Regarding the shameful brutalities of race.

If it matters to you to have truth on your
    side,
Racism in this country cannot be denied.
From its beginning, this nation was not
    for all.

Before it was founded, there had been a
    great fall.

When all of God's children can finally
    breathe free,
We can celebrate being a true democracy.
Imagine the joy and delight we will share,
When we recover the oneness already there.

Koolibah, Koolibah
(In response to "When All Africans Could
    Fly" by Langston Hughes and Arne
    Bontemps)

Koolibah, Koolibah everybody
Let those in bondage get ready to fly
The God who made us demands our
    release
Unfurl your wings and head for the sky

Though we were made from the dust of
    the earth
We were not meant to be bound to the
    ground
Gravity was not sent to make us slaves
But to anchor us as we're glory bound

This land has been mean to Africa's kin
Seeing them as property—things to own
In the eyes of God, it's an awful sin
How it cripples us all, will soon be known

Meanwhile, keep on listening for "Koolibah"
The system of slavery cannot win
The day of deliverance can't be that far
God has spoken, let Jubilee begin.

Community—Humanity at Its Best

Barricades and bunkers
Boundaries and borders
Function to separate
Foods and fashions
Mountains and rivers
Serve to segregate

Gestures and greeting styles may bespeak
    ethnicity
what we espouse and our culture allows
    and says who is free
Character is revealed in the way we seek
    pleasure
Integrity is more difficult to measure

That's why our ancestors have a message
    for us today
Don't let isolation lead to death and decay
Our species is a remarkable family
Community enriches our humanity.

"THE HEAVENS ARE telling the glory of God and the firmament proclaims (God's) handiwork. Day to day pours forth speech and night to night declares knowledge. There is no speech, nor are there words: their voice is not heard; yet their voice goes through all the earth and their words to the end of the world" (Psalm 19:1–4). I inquired about the message the heavens sought to share with us. This is what I experienced and the song I wrote in response to my question:

Song of the Heavens

What are the heavens telling us?
What truth does the cosmos convey?
What intimations are found in creation?
The sounds and the silences,
What do they say?

(Chorus)
The heavens are saying we all are one—

The earth, the sky, and the stars above.
When we care for one another
As sister, as brother,

We glorify our God who created us for
love.

Ponder the union of time and space
Observe how the galaxies dance.
Some species flourish that others be
nourished;
Could such cosmic synergy be only
chance?

(Chorus)
This is the call of the Universe:
Behold what a wonder are we
Love is the mystery shaping our destiny
Weaving connections of all things that be.

(Chorus)
The heavens are saying we all are one—
The earth, the sky, and the stars above.
When we care for one another
As sister, as brother,
We glorify our God who created us for
love.

Woe unto Those Who Desecrate the Earth

Woe unto those who desecrate the earth
With harsh lines of division and mean
    wills of separation
And treat land, sea, and air
As disposable waste dumps

Weep bitter tears of lamentation
You who sift people into races
And quarantine and neglect the undeserving
While protecting those deemed worthy of
    special care

For God sees what we do to our siblings
Sons and daughters of the one and only
And vows not to cease the labor of love
Until all creation knows we are one.

Other Wonders of the World

Other lists had to be made
Because in Divine Wisdom
God made arrangements for
Duplications and iterations
Just in case the wonders

Observed and taken notice of or
Left out other mighty acts
Of nature and her fellow artists.
So let it be known everywhere
The list of wonders of the world
Will be amended and extended
As long as we have eyes to see
And the will to explore and adore.
What a wonderful world and
what marvelous gifts God has given us
And that's the greatest wonder of all.

MY LIFE HAS been and is dedicated to "the spiritual renewal of the nation," and since I retired from Riverside Church, I embarked on the further fulfillment of that part of my calling by founding Healing of the Nations Foundation (HON) a national nonprofit, faith-based corporation that creates transformative dialogues and events to heal the wounds of racial, religious, and economic injustice festering in our nation. The goal is to unite the beloved community everywhere. I work to be inclusive of everyone because we are all God's children. While I have now come full circle, back to the area of my birthplace in North Carolina, my time in New York City was instrumental in broadening my perspective of all people.

It's a fascinating thing where I live now. I look out my window down on the North Carolina State Capitol building and the State Legislature. Every day I look out my window and from right there I feel like I see from a powerful perch. I look out another window from my home and I see where the Woolworth's lunch counter used to be. As a matter of fact, it was the same Woolworth's that inspired my poem about the segregated lunch counter. From yet another window in my home, I'm reminded of the Piggly Wiggly supermarket that was on the corner. There was also a donut shop, which had a sign that said, "As you go through life my brother but ere maybe your goal, keep your eye on the donut and not on the hole."

So, things are not that bad. I experienced coming back to North Carolina as coming back to a state where the legislature through stealthy operations took over the state with Republicans and that many Black people in this state, as I have met them, seem to have bought into a contract it seems.

Right now, in North Carolina, the contract appears to suggest, if you're Black and you want to live in North Carolina, you can have a good house, a good job, and a good reputation, as long as you keep your mouth shut. Do not seek to disturb the status quo. So far as I can see, many of our citizens buy into that contract. They have relinquished the freedom to have their say, and it is also clear that voter suppression is alive and well here. Gerrymandering has had its effect, and the best jobs are given to white people through networking of friends and family. The old neighborhoods downtown have been forced out to other places, we don't even know where. The needy have been positioned neatly hidden behind barricades of indifference. The culture is articulated, created, and manifested though the language.

So, when I talk about returning to North Carolina, it seems to suggest that after having traveled the globe as a whole man, I have returned to a place where I am still only recognized as three-fifths of a man. For Black and brown people there is no presumption of equality, and anything less than equality is odious to my spirit. Even the advantages that I have, if they are advantages, are at the discretion of others. The idea of being in a place of less than equal troubles me, and it's not that New York was the Kingdom of God either, but that returning home makes me more aware of it now.

I am capable of positive sentiments, but at the end of the day an undercurrent of disquietude travails until the last remnants of racist values have been addressed. That is why after I came back to North Carolina I picked up a special project, and that project is to try to help North Carolina recover.

North Carolina has justification for calling itself "First in Freedom"; that is what the North Carolina driver's license used to say. Now it states, "First in Flight," which is from the Wright Brothers' experience, but I want to see North Carolina become "First in Freedom" again. "First in Freedom" goes back to the Mecklenburg Resolution of 1775. In Mecklenburg County, even before the thirteen original states declared their freedom from the Crown, North Carolina was first in that declaration. I'm back here with the desire to see North Carolina decide, OK we choose to represent our freedom. It is in the DNA of our state to be free. Think about this, before we were even the United States, before the thirteen original colonies had made that declaration of freedom from the Crown, North Carolina had declared their freedom. So, there is an impulse in our DNA. I would like to see us become "First in Freedom" again, but this time for all people.

When I returned to my hometown, I convened a meeting of clergy at the Sheraton and I invited the governor, and C. K. Butterfield, and Congressman Price to come to talk to us about my vision of helping North Carolina become "First in Freedom" again—by which I said, let's make this state the first state to declare that the heritage of racial separation would be eliminated and that we would become the first state to decide we want to make this a place where citizenship is beyond the categories of class and race, to honor equal citizenship. This is to have all the rights and privileges without consideration of your ethnicity. I hope to continue to make progress in this area, but until progress is a reality and success is exemplified by making all citizens feel whole, I believe I have returned to North Carolina, the place I call home, and the feeling of being three-fifths of a man is still lingering in the air. It is not a feeling of peace, but I hope for a new day.

Oh freedom, oh freedom, oh freedom of
> mine,
Before I be a slave
I'll be buried in my grave
and go home to my God
and be free.

A Little Bit of Heaven
(My Ode to North Carolina)

A little bit of heaven in my own hometown.
Who would have thought such could be
> found?
Came back for a visit, now I want to stay
> awhile,
So many friendly faces with that million-
> dollar smile.

Like the song reminds us, "nothing could
> be finer"
Than spending some time in North
> Carolina.
No matter where you're from or where
> you were born,
You'll love our hush puppies, greens, and
> corn.

> Regardless of your background, whatever
>   your style,
> Being in Carolina will make you smile.
> A little bit of heaven and the Carolina blue,
> Will lift your spirit and comfort you.
>
> Take time to travel from the mountains to
>   the sea.
> You're bound to find a place you're gonna
>   want to be.
> So many decent people with a human touch,
> You won't be able to leave, you'll love it so
>   much.
>
> Lord, give us the humanity
> to see all colors and tribes
> are one family, as we learn
> to share together
> in peace and in spirit
> hate and violence will cease.
> That's what I'm looking for
> in this place I call home
> shall become an authentic
> Peace.

I've described the night during tobacco season when I was young, that while I was in the barn feeding wood to a furnace, curing tobacco from green to yellow to brown, I saw a most interesting sequence of events. In the light of the flames flickering forth from the furnace, I saw a cricket hurriedly scurrying along that threshing floor. A frog quickly hopped to the cricket, flicked out in a flash his long tongue and swallowed the cricket. Out of nowhere—and almost simultaneously—a Parmelee snake swallowed whole the frog that had just swallowed the cricket!

I don't know what that cricket's last meal was, but, in this world, there's a whole lot of swallowing up going on.

Where I live in Raleigh today, I can look out of my window, and I can see the Woolworth lunch counter. My brother and the students at Shaw University had had a sit-in protest at Woolworth's when, finally, the ruling came that the counter could be opened for the first time after all these years. If I wanted a sandwich at Woolworth's, I had to get it at the window, but the ruling came down that those public accommodations had to be available to all people.

So that first day when I went in to get my first sandwich—sitting down at the counter of Woolworth's—I already knew what I was going to get.

EPILOGUE

I have returned home to North Carolina. The living is quiet. Our people have been lulled to sleep. During this time in our world, our communities' things are uncertain. I believe God is still working and we will certainly hold on to our faith, hope, and love of a better tomorrow. I would like to close this work with a prophetic prayer.

> *If my people, who are called by my name, shall humble themselves, and pray, and seek my face, and turn from their wicked ways; then will I hear from heaven, and will forgive their sin, and will heal their land.*
>
> —Second Chronicles 7:14 (KJV)

O God, forgive our evil transgressions
Though we see no need to make confessions
For blocking the truth of your Sovereignty
And robbing others of their dignity.

When accused of wrongs, we are so ashamed
We find others to attack and to blame
Lies have hardened our hearts and warped
    our minds
Convincing us we are God's special kind.

Some believe they are on earth to control
To enslave others in a servant's role
Creating the scourge of domination
Which God sees as an abomination.

We spoiled nature and the rest of creation
We deserve God's judgment and
    damnation
But because You love us despite our sin
Forgive us and help us to begin again.

Call the races together to repent
And to accept the mission God has sent:
To use our power to help God repair
The damage humans have done
    everywhere.

In Your Name we pray
Amen.

Go Forth
(A Benediction)

Go forth in the Name of the Lord
To spread glad tidings abroad
The love that you share
And the witness you bear
Will bring honor and glory to God.

Go forth with a joyful Amen!
Until we gather again
Remember the word
Your spirit has heard
"God's Love is the hope of the world."

ACKNOWLEDGMENTS

MY FIRST WORDS of gratitude for assistance in completing this volume of poems goes to God, who sparked my imagination and even gave the thoughts and expressions found in these pages. Sometimes I was awakened in the middle of the night, or while I was reading verses of Scripture, the inspiration came.

In the midst of a counseling session out of the blue, a nugget of wisdom would spring forth, marinate for a while, and then find a form that captured the essence of truth sent for that moment. Often a dictionary search for the rhyming words or the apt image would lead to the pearl of great price.

There is a list of professional colleagues or clergy friends who were the first to read my poetry and prose. I may have forgotten the names of some folks, but I want to be sure to include the following: Edie Beaujon, Katherine Henderson, Johnetta B. Cole, Marion Wright Edelman, Eyvonne Delk, Clarence Newsome, Brad Braxton, Karen Leahy, Walter Brueggerman, Jim Wallis, Cornel West, Elroy Lewis, Jeremiah Wright, Bishop William Barber, Iva Carruthers, Ian Straker, Gail Wright Sirmans, Sujay Johnson Cook, Julie Johnson Staples, Evelyn Davis, Eugene Palmore, Ellen Davis, Luke Powery, William Turner, Regina Graham, Barbara George, Walter Wink, Oliver Wells, Bishop Johnny Ray Youngblood, Alonzo Wyatt, Glenn Smith, Carrie Bolton, Nancy Sehested, Dumas Harshaw, Otis Moss III, Jessie Williams, Kimberly Jordan, Gary Simpson, Colita Fairfax, Richard Berman, Jim Clark, Linda Tarry-Chard, Perry and Leah Berkowitz, Keith Reinhart, Mary Stanton, Sarah Lewis, John and Nikki McClusky, Paul Nichols, Clair Rosenfield, Carrie Jackson, Bishop Michael Curry, Irving Stubbs, James Melvin Washington, Chang Park, Jesse Jackson Jr., Margo Fish, and Robert Seymour.

April L. Smith of the KinZac Group has served as a God-appointed midwife on this volume. She has been a remarkable literary agent, theological consultant, and navigator through the swirling waters of book publication. A special thanks to her daughter and personal assistant Kinnidy D. Coley as well. I dare not neglect to mention the eloquent words of those who wrote endorsements for this work and the staff of Broadleaf Books who poured into the editing of this work as if it were their very own child. Special thanks to Adrienne Ingrum who was determined to bring this work forward. I must give thanks to the congregations who raised me in faith and character and the many students and teachers who, through the years, have given me many precious theological insights.

My parents, Bishop James A. Forbes Sr. and Mrs. Mabel Clemmons Forbes, must receive the highest appreciation. They were not only the biological source of my being but the spiritual origin of all that I have become. My surviving siblings have served as an unofficial editorial board of my sermons and all my writings. Thanks go to them and their spouses and children, who meet on a family call every Tuesday at 2:00 pm to ensure that all is well with each of us. It is true for me what my African ancestors taught us to say, "I am because we are."

For sixty years, Bettye Franks Forbes has been my loving wife and partner in ministry and has proven to be more than my better half. Whatever accolades are sent my way, be sure to give my lover her share. Many thanks to my son, James A. Forbes III, as he is trying to care for a nearly 90-year-old preacher.

When all is said and done, I humbly dedicate this work to my parents, wife, son, and family.

INDEX OF NAMES

Abram, 31, 187
Adams, Diane (Mrs. Bert Adams), 93
Ahab, 32

Boesak, Alan, 117
Bontemps, Arne, 190
Butterfield, C. K., 200

Callender, Eugene, 71–72
Clark, Linda, 122
Clements, William, 111
Clemons, Ada, 7
Clemons, O. C., 6–7, 11
Clemons, Rosa, 7
Coffin, William, 135
Cone, James, 114–16

Dunn, James D. G., 127

Einstein, Albert, 153
Eisenhower, Dwight D., 126
Elijah, 31
Ellison, Ralph, 93
Esther, 185

Fletcher, John Caldwell, 119
Floyd, George, 87
Forbes III, James A., 119
Forbes, Anna (sister), 35
Forbes, Anna Little, 3
Forbes, Charlie, 3
Forbes, David, 33, 34, 81
Forbes, Evangeline, 33
Forbes, James Alexander, Sr., 3–7, 23, 63, 79, 98, 122
Forbes, Mabel Clemons, 3, 11–13, 15–16, 23, 39–40, 56–58

Index of Names

Forbes, Malcolm, 7
Forbes, Robert, 8
Fosdick, Harry Emerson, 136
Franks, Bettye (Bettye Forbes), 101–2, 107, 113

Graham, Billy, 131

Helms, Jesse, 26
Holton, Anne, 112
Holton, Linwood, 111–12
Hughes. Langston, 190

Isaiah, 43–44

Jesus Christ, 14, 17–18, 26, 94–95, 115–16, 145, 176
Job, 185
Jones, Miles, 114

Kaine, Tim, 112
Kelsey, George, 86–87
Kiepper, Alan F., 112
King, Martin Luther, Jr., 34, 39–40, 56–59, 73, 114, 116–17, 120, 131, 159, 185
Kovel, Joel, 128–29

Lassiter, Mother, 15
Lawson, Equilla, 43–44
Lawson, Warner, 38
Lincoln, Abraham, 183
Lowe, Walter Edison, 154

Marcus, Dorothy, 85–86
Marney, Carlisle, 80
Mary, 47–48

Mayo, Paul M., 126
Mitchell, Henry, 114–15

Naomi, 109–10
Nichols, Paul, 115
Niebuhr, Reinhold, 67

Ormandy, Eugene, 44

Parsons, Mr. and Mrs., 5–6
Paul, 127
Perry, Nelson, 37
Perry, Susie Vick, 37
Peter, Saint, 144
Price, David E., 200

Robinson, James Herman, 71
Rockefeller, John D., 126, 136
Rovelli, Carlo, 153
Ruth, 109–10

Seymour, Robert, 92–93
Shapiro, Harold, 135–36
Shinn, Roger, 69
Shriver, Don and Peggy, 122–23
Smith, John E., 63
Sullivan, Leon, 114

Taylor, Gardner, 124
Tchaikovsky, Pyotr Ilyich, 44
Till, Emmett, 93
Tillich, Paul, 99
Trump, Donald, 73

Van Dusen, Henry Pitney, 66

Walker, Madam C. J., 104
Williamson, Mother, 15